CELEBRITY SERVICE

Secret Sauce

GEOFF RAMM

CELEBRITY SERVICE SECRET SAUCE

ISBN 978-1-917490-18-4

Published in 2026 by Right Book Press
Printed in the UK in December 2025

Manufactured by
Sue Richardson Associates Ltd.
Studio 6,
9, Marsh Street
Bristol
BS1 4AA
info@therightbookcompany.com

What they say...
ENDORSEMENTS

" *Geoff Ramm's Celebrity Service message resonated deeply with our organisation, causing an immediate shift in our organisation's customer focus that remains today. I've seen countless speakers over the years, but none have been like Geoff – read this book if you want to know how the customer service magic happens.*

Christian Hunter, managing director, Travellers Choice, Australia

" *Geoff Ramm's engaging style and real-life examples encourage people to think differently and take their own action. After reading this, you'll be having many a light bulb moment!*

Tracey Powers, UK sales director, Avon

" *Geoff Ramm's infectious energy, captivating real-world examples and signature 'Celebrity Service' mindset will leave you thinking bigger, acting bolder and delivering exceptional experiences for your customers. This has the potential for massive impact across the UK's business community and beyond.*

Jan Brumby, CEO, For Entrepreneurs Only

" *Thanks to Geoff Ramm, we're always looking out for examples of Celebrity Service. We've changed the way we do things to make interactions with our business more fun and memorable, and the feedback has been fantastic!*

Rachel Smurthwaite, head of communications, Sewell Group

About GEOFF

Forbes magazine called him 'a game changer'. You might think of him as the world's most inspirational customer service speaker. Geoff Ramm is the creator and author of Celebrity Service, Celebrity Service Superstars and now Celebrity Service Secret Sauce.

He loves to inspire high-performance teams, entrepreneurs and organisations to deliver incredible customer experiences.

He loves to see the results that his keynotes and interactive sessions bring.

He loves catching people delivering wonderful experiences.

He loves putting those people on a pedestal and amplifying their brilliance in books, podcasts and from the stage.

He loves his football team and a stadium tour or three.

He still loves his galaxy far, far away.

He still loves his cider but is drifting more towards spiced rum and Pepsi these days.

Most importantly, he loves his Rammlings and this book is dedicated to them... Hayley, Grace and Elliot xxx

CONTENTS

Mixing The INGREDIENTS

"YOUR GREATEST MARKETING TOMORROW IS THE SERVICE YOU DELIVER TODAY."

GEOFF RAMM

The Story SO FAR...

My breakthrough book, *Celebrity Service*, revealed for the very first time (on a page) the philosophy that showed the 'gap in your customer service you never knew existed'.

It challenged readers' thinking and created a mindset to a completely new, refreshing and, dare I say, exciting way of delivering a better customer service experience.

It highlighted the nine core areas of CELEBRITY (Consistency, Excitement, Love, Engagement, Bravado, Response, Independence, Thank You and You, Your Team) and showed readers how to embark on embracing and delivering this philosophy in any business or organisation.

Then along came Celebrity Service Superstars, which was an explosion of technicolour treats, with additional superstar interviews from some of the amazing people I've had the pleasure of meeting along the way.

As well as the new stories, there were also brand new 120 Challenges (for more about these, see page 29) to enhance your service creativity.

Both books received wonderful reviews, and for that I am eternally grateful and proud. The books regularly pop up on social media posts as go-to publications when you're in need of inspiration for a great customer service idea or three.

So many of the posts I've been tagged into feature the books on someone's desk or a team holding them. Then there were the photos taken on holiday, with the books resting on someone's lap by the pool or on a far-flung beach. However, the best one was from my youngest ever reader, Milo, with his dad Alexander. They were reading it in the labour ward of a hospital.

So, after experiencing many amazing Celebrity Service moments (and some horrendous ones, too), after many speaking trips, arduous train journeys and sitting in departure lounges, the burning question throughout has been…

Should I? Shouldn't I? Write the next book?

The answer is, of course, yes (which you already knew, as you are holding the book right now). I have so many more stories that I share from the stage, and now I want everyone to read them. I have witnessed some truly amazing people along the way, whether through work or play.

So here it is, the third instalment of Celebrity Service. The trilogy, as it were, is now complete (for more details about the first two books, see page 163).

I really hope you enjoy it. I hope it will inspire you and your team to once again go on to discover the gap in your service you never knew existed.

But alongside these brand-new stories and techniques, there has to be a twist, so here it is…

What Exactly is... CELEBRITY SERVICE?

If you haven't read my first two books, watched any of the videos or been in the audience at one of my conferences, then let me briefly explain what Celebrity Service is all about.

Quite simply, it's the gap in your service you never knew existed.

You see, I'd hazard a guess that you and your team are pretty good at delivering customer service. In fact, if I were to ask you right now, on a scale of 1 to 10, where 1 is awful and 10 is incredible, (from more than two decades of asking this question) you and the majority of the clients I work with will say they are a 7 or 8 out of 10. On the odd occasion, there will be 4s and 5s and maybe the odd 9 or 10, but my research reveals that the vast majority of people will rate themselves as a 7 to 8 – not the lowest nor the highest, but in those upper reaches, while admitting there is room for improvement.

Which brings me to my next question: 'Where does that improvement come from?'

I have no idea how many customer service speakers you've seen in your career, how many customer service training days you've had to endure, how many books you've read or service manuals you've flicked through, but in order for you and your business to truly stand out from the competition, almost every speaker, trainer, book and manual will tell you there are two things that need to happen for you to become number one in your sector for customer service experience.

The first one is: you must always go the extra...

Yes, you guessed it... mile.

The second is: you must always exceed...

Yes, you've got this one right, too... expectations.

Now, if you were to walk back into your workplace to inspire your team to deliver a real game-changing service experience, could you imagine the look on their faces if you were to tell them to 'go the extra mile' or 'exceed expectations'?

We have trotted out these phrases for decades.

There's nothing new in the world of customer service.

But that's about to change.

With just one question, you can transform your service levels, forever. This one question is the philosophy, and here it is...

If your next customer were to call you, arrange an appointment, email you, walk into your business tomorrow, and they were an A-list, Hollywood, Bollywood, movie, musical, sporting god or goddess...

What would you say?

What would you do?

How would you react?

What would be the difference?

If they requested a proposal, I wonder how long it would take you to send it over?

If they entered your workplace for a meeting, I wonder how clean and tidy your desk would be?

I wonder what you would wear? And would your smile be the widest it's ever been?

What refreshments would you serve?

When they drove outside your building, would they find it hard to park? Or would you do something to help?

When you emailed back, I wonder if you ditched your template response for something more personalised?

Which words would you choose in that email, voicemail or message to create a greater service experience?

Quite simply, if an A-list celebrity were to become your next colleague, customer, member, client, passenger or guest, everything about your service levels would change. And for change, see improve; and for improvement, you and your team can discover the gap in your service you never knew existed.

If you can fill this gap, it will ensure the competition can never touch you for customer service.

But wanting to deliver Celebrity Service is a choice.

So, choose well.

Adding The
SECRET SAUCE

"UP YOUR GAME OR PLAY THE SAME."

GEOFF RAMM

What is...
CELEBRITY SERVICE SECRET SAUCE?

Let me take you back to your earliest memory of audible excitement – the sound of a musical jingle playing in an ice cream van far off in the distance.

You couldn't see it, but you could hear it. It was a muffled, cheery tune and you knew that, as it got louder, it wouldn't be long before the van was here.

Like the products inside the van, you instantly froze. You and your friends would give each other a knowing look and, without saying a word, run off in different directions, into your homes, to grab your pocket money, run back to the path, stand by the kerb and wait.

'The ice cream van is here!'

You chose your ice cream. You paid your money. The experience was real.

When it came to the ice cream itself, let's face it, the cone was the boring part. However, that waffle or sugar cone base held everything in place.

Then there was the ice cream. Would you go for whippy, soft vanilla or a more adventurous flavour? These were the high-stakes decisions you had to make as a child. Get that right and the next ten minutes would be heaven; make a wrong choice and you'd have to wait another week for the sound of the van's jingle.

But that's not all. Before you handed over your money, you'd be asked one life-changing question…

'Would you like monkey's blood?'

If you are from the North East, those last two words make perfect sense. For anyone outside of our borders, please do not be afraid. No monkeys were harmed in the making of this ice cream and, as far as I know, blood was never spilled on my ice cream.

Monkey's blood is the rather alarming term for what is essentially strawberry sauce. I believe the term originated in Sunderland.

This final ingredient completes the ice cream.

It's the one thing that makes the difference.

It's the final thing, this one last ingredient that completes the experience.

In the parallel world of business, you have your base, you have a foundation that holds everything together (the cone), you have the main products or services that people are buying (the ice cream).

BUT WHAT'S THE ONE THING THAT MAKES THE DIFFERENCE TO YOUR BUSINESS TO COMPLETE THE EXPERIENCE?

Let's face it, all airlines take you from departure to arrivals, but some do it so much better.

Hotels check you in and check you out, but some do it so much better.

Taxi drivers pick you up and drop you off, but some do it so much better.

Universities enrol you and pass you out at graduation, but some do it so much better.

But what is better? What do they add? What's the special ingredient? What is their Secret Sauce?

In creating that special something, you create differentiation in the marketplace – through your product, or through the team that deliver the service.

But some do it better than others. While some offer a bland, run-of- the-mill experience, others leave you salivating at the gills, wanting more. Which begs the question, why do so many offer such a bland, run-of-the-mill service that mirrors their competitors?

Q: So what will you become?

A: Become a game changer of service!

So what's the one thing you can add to really make the difference?

What's the one thing that could really make your customer experience pop?

What's the one thing you can do that people will remember you for?

What's the one thing you do for your team that makes your business a great place to work?

What's that delicious Secret Sauce that will set you apart?

For some, their Secret Sauce could be their speed of response. For others, it could be their attention to detail. Or maybe it's the high degree of personalisation. How about the packaging? How about making life easier when your customer needs to return your product? How about that onboarding experience for your future colleague? Or the thing you do when a teammate goes on or returns from maternity or paternity leave? Maybe it's the way you handle customer disappointment and complaints. Maybe it's creating something that the competition can't. It could be remembering important details.

Or maybe, with the help of this book, you can go a little deeper.

So... WHAT'S NEW

This book will explore those Secret Sauce moments – those tiny, minuscule things that make you memorable, referable and talked about for decades to come.

It will feature some amazing yet simple ideas and stories from my speaking travels, our family breaks and all-round observations that have made me smile, laugh or rage from a passionate service perspective.

We're going to go on another journey, from stadium tours to baggage carousels, from taxi rides to ordering food and from cinema trips to comedy shows. Grab your visas, ESTAs and passports as we take in the sights and sounds of Chicago and Madrid, New York and Paris, and travel from Tamworth to Rome. Once again, it's time to be inspired.

INTERACTIVE FEATURES

When you see the QR Code -Simply scan and immerse yourself in the world of Geoff's secret sauce moments.

120 CHALLENGES ARE BACK

There will, of course, be some brand new 120 Challenges to test you and your team's creativity in generating ideas the world will talk about.

EXPERIENCE MAKERS

For the very first time, the book will also feature my Experience Makers team challenges, to challenge and inspire you and your colleagues to generate wonderful customer experiences.

But will there be any more Star Wars stories, I hear you ask?

You'll have to wait and see...

There is...
ALWAYS A
DIFFERENCE

'Oh, but we treat everyone the same, Geoff.'

'We wouldn't treat anyone any differently if they were a celebrity or not.'

'Everyone receives the same high level of service from us.'

On the very rare occasion when I am challenged by someone who says they wouldn't treat a celebrity any differently to a regular customer, I say with a wry smile, 'Nope, wrong, incorrect and simply not true.'

Celebrity Service changes everything about you. It changes your thinking as a team and your strategy for your organisation. With a wider smile and our hearts beating faster, you will always deliver something greater than before. The whole philosophy of Celebrity Service is about knowing what you would do to deliver a greater experience, and then doing it for everyone. This is the key that unlocks your competitive advantage.

If you are still unsure that a Celebrity Service gap exists, then let me reveal this wonderful list of A-list delights…

WHAT IS IT? SOME KIND OF LOCAL TROUBLE?

The news broke on 8 June 2021. I remember it vividly. A wave of euphoria, excitement and disbelief swept across the north-east of England. Radio stations, TV crews, news reporters and social media were on high alert as someone was spotted cycling along North Shields Fish Quay. A day later, this same someone was spotted walking along the Quayside in Newcastle upon Tyne. And, lo and behold, this same person had the audacity to have lunch at a local restaurant.

This wasn't any normal cyclist, walker or person fancying something to eat. This was Han, Indiana and Dr Kimble all rolled into one. Yes, that's right, Harrison Ford was in town. Captain Solo was just ten miles from my home!!! Mr Ford was here filming Indiana Jones and the Dial of Destiny at the stunning Bamburgh Castle in Northumberland. The news of his sighting swept across social media in seconds, and later that day became the number one news story on both local BBC and ITV news channels.

'Harrison Watch' had begun. Where was he now? Where was he staying? Who did he meet and what did he say?

First, the news broke at the Ship's Cat in North Shields, where a customer took to social media to report:

'Imagine sitting here enjoying your coffee, then you look over and it's… Indiana Jones! What an honour to have Harrison Ford join us today on the decking here at the Ship's Cat! You are welcome back anytime. What a legend!'

Imagine how excited the customers and staff must have been!

Harrison was staying at the wonderful Malmaison hotel in Newcastle, and also popped into the Khai Khai restaurant, where he was asked to pose for a picture. This was liked and shared like crazy on the restaurant's social channels.

I wonder whether the chef double or triple checked his order before it left the kitchen that day? I wonder if the waiting staff had bigger smiles on their faces? I wonder if they heightened their level of service that day? And if Harrison had asked for something they didn't have on the menu, would they have run to the local shop to get it for him? We may never know.

The Ford frenzy lasted for a few more days until he took a helicopter to Pinewood Studios to continue filming the all-action blockbuster. And life in the North East resumed to pre-'Harrison Watch' levels.

There is always a difference.

DOWNGRADED

Picture the scene. You are travelling from South Africa to the UK, and then onto the United States. It's a long, long-haul flight, but thankfully you have purchased a business class ticket, so you can sit back, recline and relax.

However, when you arrive at check-in, you are told you have been downgraded. Imagine your disbelief. Imagine your anger. Imagine you just happened to be a famous comedian and you were itching to share this story on your Netflix shows and worldwide tours.

This actually happened to one of my favourite comedians, the side-splitting storyteller, Jim Jefferies. I was listening to the Australian comic's BARE tour, and his closing story on stage was all about his downgraded experience. It would be unfair of me to recount the story for you here, as only Jim can do it justice with his genius delivery.

Instead, I urge you to search for 'Downgraded' online. Jefferies makes 'a beautiful noise' about how poorly he and many other passengers were treated (trust me, it has a hilarious ending). Warning: there is very strong language throughout, but I promise it's worth it.

There used to be a lovely saying many moons ago: receive good service and someone will tell three people; receive poor service and that person will tell ten. I wonder how many views and listeners this story has had? And I dare say there will be a few more now that you've put this book down to watch or listen to the story on your phone.

Even in the world of Celebrity Service, there is a hierarchy of what we will and won't do for a customer. Jim Jefferies is a celebrity, but along came a bigger one to bump him off the flight.

There is always a difference.

THE WONDER OF WREXHAM

QUESTION 1: **Who was the manager of Wrexham AFC when they were promoted to the English Football League in 2023? (1pt)**

QUESTION 2: **Wrexham beat Boreham Wood 3-1 to clinch promotion, but can you name their two goal scorers? (2pts)**

QUESTION 3: **Who are the two owners of Wrexham AFC? (2pts)**

If you are a Wrexham fan, congratulations – you've probably scored a maximum of five points. If you are reading this book anywhere else in the world, then you have probably scored two points. I am guessing most of you knew at least one of the answers to Question 3.

The footballing world was turned on its head in 2021 when Hollywood stars Ryan Reynolds and Rob McElhenney took over the reins of the National League side, Wrexham AFC. It's a true Tinseltown tale of how the celebrity duo brought their passion, publicity and oodles of investment to a lower league team in North Wales. They also embraced the community, the culture and even its language. They went on to create their own Disney+ documentary, *Welcome to Wrexham* (If you've not seen it, it's brilliant).

Due to the high-profile takeover and connections, TikTok became the club's shirt sponsors and Expedia soon followed. The whole town was swept up in the euphoria that pretty much only A-list celebrities can bring. The wave of positivity, excitement and hope was palpable. It was wonderful to watch the story unfold and see the faces of a community smile in unison after decades of disappointment.

While Harrison Ford attracted regional publicity in the North East, Ryan and Rob had a global spotlight thrust upon them. However, the narrative focuses on them, as the media are, of course, excited by the presence of Hollywood celebrities. In every interview, every mention, it is rarely the team, the manager or the coach that receives the plaudits. On the day that Wrexham were promoted to the English Football League, the BBC headlines read: 'Welsh win promotion to EFL with Hollywood actors watching' and 'Hollywood glitter helps Wrexham to promotion glory'.

They have since gone on to become the first club to achieve back-to-back-to-back promotions. And who knows, by the time you are reading this, they could have won the Premier League and Champions League!

It's a fantastic sporting fairy tale.

But remember, there is always a difference.

HADDOCK FOR HENDRIX?

If you should ever visit the wonderful seaside village of Tynemouth and you happen to say to yourself, 'Oh, I'd love some fish and chips', then let me introduce you to Marshall's, also known as 'the Fryery by the Priory'. This fish and chip restaurant is a wonderful place. I remember visiting it as a child, and I still visit now. The queues out of the narrow doorway are as long as the cod they serve, and

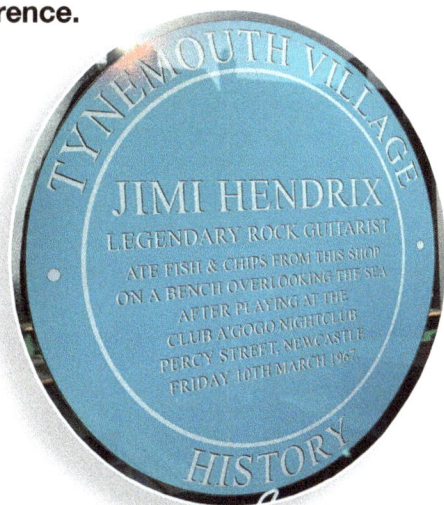

there's a very good reason why. They are salt and vinegar-tastic!

However, on 10 May 1967, seven years before I was born, one special customer paid them a visit. This customer received their newspaper-wrapped fish and chips and sat on a bench overlooking the North Sea. How do I know this? Well, because it is proudly displayed on the window of the restaurant for everyone to admire.

There is always a difference.

SIGN YOUR NAME

The amazing Porsche Experience Centre adjoins the iconic Silverstone racetrack in Towcester. Anyone can book an experience, which puts your driving skills to the test under the watchful eye of a professional driver. My experience lasted 90 minutes and I left the 911 supercar with my knees knocking and my hands still in white-knuckle grip mode. It's exhilarating and breathtaking (if you like that sort of thing). Leaving your vehicle, you walk back into the main building, where you can view some stunning vintage Porsches, grab some refreshments and relax after your breakneck session. But just as you walk through the doors, there is a wall in front of you, covered in signatures. People who'd been through the experience had signed their names on the bright, white wall.

I looked for a pen, thinking that everyone who takes part in this experience signs their name as they leave. There was no pen. I was wrong. You see, this wall is a Wall of Fame – where only celebrities get the chance to sign their names. I had a good look, trying to find people I may have heard of, and managed to decipher the scribblings of legendary Team GB cyclists Sir Chris Hoy, Sir Jason Kenny and Dame Laura Kenny, as well as the rock god himself, Brian Johnson, lead singer of AC/DC.

There is always a difference.

A Few
RAMMBLINGS...

Before we move on to the stories and ideas, here are a few thoughts, observations and head-in-hands moments from the world of customer service.

Customer expectations are at an all-time high.

We are slowly replacing hearts and eyes with scans and clicks.

We are quick to complain and slow to congratulate.

Prices are rising while service is slipping.

We try to pay with cash and it's card only.

We try to pay with a card and it's cash only.

Front-line staff are at the coal face, overwhelmed and underprepared.

It's easy to subscribe and buy, but we have to enter the Crystal Maze to leave.

There's an infatuation with and over-reliance on technology.

Robots are asking humans if they are robots.

Speaking to an actual human has become obsolete.

I'm all for making life and service easy for the customer, but we are replacing human interaction with downloadable (if you have Wi-Fi) apps on your phone.

Oh, and don't get me started on self-service supermarket checkouts. I've spent so much time waiting for someone to check my unexpected item in the bagging area that some of the items passed their sell-by date by the time I'd left.

Progress? When the customer receives an inferior service than they previously enjoyed, then, no – you have regressed.

I'm all for improvement of service design, but when profits come before people, customer service suffers.

Read this last sentence again.

And again.

We are ever so slowly losing the art of interaction, engagement and conversation, or something I'd call the cornerstone of a successful Celebrity Service experience.

So we must be careful.

We must strike a balance, with the customer at the heart of everything we do.

Artificial intelligence (AI) must be efficient. Human intelligence (HI) must be exquisite.

And it's never too late to stop, think and reimagine a service experience the world will talk about.

WHAT DO YOU DO, GEOFF?

I'd like to think I deliver a great service, but I always know there's room for improvement at any client touchpoint.

Since launching my business on 1 March 2002, I have constantly striven to improve everything I do. Not just delivering on stage or with my marketing materials – I mean the service I give to clients. And even when you already stand out from your competitors, I know it can always be improved upon over time.

Let me share a couple of examples…

BECOMING THE NEXT MILK TRAY MAN...

When I arrive at an event, I always have a gift in my hand for the client who has booked me.

That gift is a box of Cadbury's Milk Tray chocolates.

WHY MILK TRAY?

When I was just six years old, I had one ambition in life: to become the next Milk Tray man. For those of you who are way too young to understand, you'll have to search for 'Milk Tray man advert' on YouTube. I used to share this story when I first started speaking as an example of a brand that stood out from the rest for its advertising and marketing.

Since 2002, on arrival, I have always handed a box of Milk Tray to the client. However, it takes a dedicated team to create a successful conference, so with that in mind, the double-layered box is not just for one person – it's for everyone to share.

Of course, I need to personalise it, so I have cards printed, then I handwrite the client's name and a 'thank you' message before glueing it in the top right-hand corner of the box.

It's just a small token of thanks, but it's my way of saying 'thank you' for choosing me and that I appreciate all their hard work and support in the lead-up to the event.

Post-Covid, most of the world seemed to be cutting back on the niceties of the service experience. So when life started to normalise and live events returned with a bang, I had to make a big business decision.

SHOULD I:

A. Stop buying 'thank you' chocolates for my clients? After all, this is a bottom-line cost!

B. Purchase the smaller, one layered, cheaper box of chocolates? It's still a nice 'thank you' gesture, but I'd save money!

C. Keep the exact same gift? (After all, clients loved it.)

WHAT WOULD YOU HAVE DONE?

In the end, I chose neither of those options and opted for:

D. Turn up to the event, find the client, reach into my laptop bag and... pull out the biggest box of Milk Tray chocolates Cadbury's sells. It's twice the size of the original box I used to gift to the client.

Of course they cost more, and they do take up more space in my case. But that's OK with me. In the grand scheme of things, a few extra pounds in cash or a few extra pounds at check-in, it really doesn't matter. What matters most is the smile on the client's face when I say, 'Thank you.'

Everything you are delivering can be improved upon.

As with any aspect of your service, there are four things you can do right now:

- Stop what you are delivering.
- Reduce what you are delivering.
- Keep it going as it is.
- Improve on it further.

The chocolates aren't the only gift at the bottom of the bag. I also wanted something that lasted longer than cocoa-infused treats – something that was cool, cute and cuddly.

INTRODUCING THE ONE AND ONLY 'LITTLE RAM'.

This gorgeous, fluffy mascot sits on your desk as a 'raminder' of your conference and to always deliver Celebrity Service.

I designed the message to read: 'PLEASE LOOK AFTER ME... and your customers'. I had it printed, then cut a strand of wool before threading it through the card to hang around Little Ram's neck.

Clients absolutely love Little Ram – almost as much as I love giving him away as a 'thank you' gift!

It may be a stuffed toy, but it's a little Secret Sauce moment that sets me apart from other speakers.

Oh, and how do I know clients love them?

Well, they give him a name. They place him around the venue or office. They take a picture and tag me in it.

I'm not saying I'm a service saint, but I can promise you I'm always thinking, always creating and hopefully always delivering.

Just like you, I'm in competition, so I want to create a great experience for my clients.

If you embrace the Celebrity Service principle, you will stand out.

Enough about Little Ram and chocolates – it's time to grab your cone, choose your ice cream and let the Secret Sauce flow in helping to inspire you and your team to become memorable, referable and talked about for decades to come.

Create
YOUR OWN
MAGIC

"ARE YOU AN ORDER TAKER OR AN EXPERIENCE MAKER?"

GEOFF RAMM

Introducing
THE 120 CHALLENGE

Can you and your team generate potentially award-winning ideas in just two minutes? It's time for the one and only 120 Challenge.

This is an amazingly creative and very easy to adopt technique that I created more than two decades ago. To complement my keynote talks, I wanted to introduce a highly interactive section that would bring about maximum engagement with any team or audience.

It needed to be quick, so two minutes was the perfect length – and 120 seconds would be challenging for everyone. The audience would have to focus on the issue, solve a problem or improve any touchpoint in a very short passage of time.

They did just that, but what I hadn't quite anticipated were the ideas that would emerge from this fully interactive creation. When I say ideas, I mean results – amazing, thoughtful ideas and cost-effective suggestions that teams and organisations had simply never come up with before.

Throughout the world and in every sector imaginable, the 120 Challenge has never failed to generate ideas and experiences teams could then use the very next day.

In short, it's a quick-fire round of pure creativity, ideas and inspiration. But the longer-term value is in giving you a technique you can easily adopt to maintain and improve Celebrity Service momentum in your business or organisation.

Take any external customer or internal colleague touchpoint, process or piece of communication, give it a 120 makeover, and you will realise that this simplest of techniques will breathe fresh, creative ideas into your business.

WHAT YOU NEED

HOW MANY CAN PLAY?

You need to work in teams. You can do this as a duet or with up to ten people per team, depending on the size of your department or business.

HOW MANY TEAMS?

There needs to be a level of competition, so try to create at least three teams. I have also done this with more than 50 teams. Warning: the more teams you have, the louder it will become, so bring your earplugs.

WHAT EQUIPMENT DO YOU NEED?

Plain paper and coloured felt tip pens, or a tablet, a stopwatch or an egg timer. Use a flipchart if you have one or just use a table to rest on.

HOW DO YOU PLAY?

Give your teams the exact same challenge – maybe something that inspired you recently. Describe the story to the teams, and without revealing the amazing piece of service or experience, ask them to figure out in 120 seconds what they would have done to improve both.

HOW IS IT TIMED?

Start the clock. Halfway through, give your teams a one-minute warning, 30 seconds warning, and then loudly count down: '5, 4, 3, 2, 1... stop! Put down your pens. Who wants to share their ideas with the room first?'

HOW DO YOU SHARE THE RESULTS?

Let every team reveal their ideas. Let everyone contribute to the challenge. Now record all of these ideas, either by taking a photograph of the papers or writing down the best ones on the board. Prizes can now be given out to the winners of most creative, most cost-effective, most crazy idea, etc.

WHAT ARE THE PRIZES?

Give your team an incentive (sweets, candies, a Celebrity Service 120 trophy, drinks vouchers, a day off work, basically anything to reward and recognise their creativity).

OBSERVATIONAL TIP

When one team reveals their answers, listen to the reaction in the room. If you hear gasps, giggles or a round of applause, this clearly resonates with your team. From this, you could take the idea and develop it further.

Once the 120 Challenge has concluded, you can reveal the ideas you received from the question you set. You see, the 120 Challenge isn't a made-up question to spark everyone's imagination, it's a real-life scenario, and this is what your teams will be inspired by the most. Real people in real situations, delivering real-life service excellence.

Now you know its origins and how you can introduce it to your business or organisation, but let me set the ball rolling for you , with the first 120 Challenge of Celebrity Service Secret Sauce…

BRINGING THE 120 CHALLENGE INTO YOUR BUSINESS

It would be a perfect match if you were to own a car dealership, restaurant or an airport lounge. Although these are all real-life examples, you also need to look at how they can benefit you, your team and your organisation.

The 120 Challenge is all about taking one touchpoint within your business and giving it the Celebrity Service treatment to develop a Secret Sauce idea or two.

To help you on your way, here are a handful of touchpoints to get your creative juices flowing.

Internal Celebrity Service (your team)

- onboarding processes
- offer of employment letter
- what can we send our future colleague a week before they arrive?
- what can we send to someone who is home working?
- recognising a long-service colleague
- celebrating our colleagues leaving on maternity and paternity leave.

External Celebrity Service (your customers)

- first visit to their place of work
- first visit to your office/place of work
- what to do when you sign the contract
- what to say or do when the project is complete
- how to keep in touch throughout the process.

Good luck.

120 Challenge
HANDOVER
HEROES

If you've ever bought a brand-new car, you'll recognise its unforgettable aroma. Like a morning frost, a sea breeze, or a walk through the Scottish Highlands, there's nothing quite like that 'new car smell'. It reminds you that everything is fresh, untouched, and it's all yours for the first time. Unfortunately, it only lasts for a few weeks, but boy, if only you could purchase this as an optional extra to have every day.

However, receiving the keys to your second most expensive purchase is often fraught with a to-do list as long as the road you are eventually going to drive on.

You may have a car to sell, either privately or as part of a trade-in, or maybe through an online provider. Making appointments, taking photos, uploading, speaking to call centres – this can be a time-consuming challenge in itself. The challenges continue if you have a private registration plate, as you will have to contact the government via their website or offices to place it on retention, while filling in forms and paying them a fee for the privilege. This sequence is then reversed if you want to put your private plate on your future car.

Then there is the list that includes taxing the vehicle and insuring it. (Wouldn't it be lovely if your current insurer did everything they could to keep you loyal? But invariably, their prices have skyrocketed within a year and now you have to research a new provider.) Now there's a system that could do with some Celebrity Service.

So there is quite a bit to do before that 'new car smell' can be inhaled.

Having navigated the process and selected the car you love, the very least any motor dealer could do would be to make the handover of your new vehicle an experience you will never forget. It would be gorgeously wrapped in so many Celebrity Service moments that you would tell your friends, your family and your work colleagues, and share them across socials for everyone to see.

This happens all of the time, yes?

If you have ever collected your brand-new car on handover day, you can age yourself by what you are about to read...

Placed on the back seat of your car is a huge bunch of flowers. (Congratulations, you are most likely to be over 40 years old.)

Or...

Placed on the back seat of your car is a bunch of... well, nothing really, not even a petal. (Congratulations, you are still young and probably under the age of 40.)

Back in the halcyon days, the bunch of flowers was seen as part of the experience. They were often purchased from a local florist and handed over with the keys. Although it was a great idea, all the dealerships copied one another, hence no one ever truly stood out. Sadly, though, this appreciative gift fell by the wayside some years ago. Dealers simply stopped doing it. Why would you create and deliver something customers loved and came to expect, and then stop? Cost? Effort? Both? Either way, the handover experience stalled, received a puncture and basically reversed itself. I felt sorry for the customer whose expectations were dashed, and the local florist who benefited from a bunch of orders every month.

You may be flowerless, but at least your brand-new car had a full tank of petrol/diesel/electric charge for you to drive away with, yes?

Hmmm... If you're lucky, you may receive half a tank at best.

As it stands today, the experience seems to rely on your new car being in the showroom with a large cloth covering it, as if some sort of magician's final act is about to take place. As you enter the presentation room, the salesperson asks if you'd like to take photos or a video and then, ever so slowly, seductively removes the cloth so you can see your brand-new car in all its shining glory. It's a wonderful moment, for sure. However, everyone has these giant cloths now and the reveals have slowly become the flowers of yesteryear.

You sign the remaining forms, sync your phone to the vehicle, and that's it – it's time to drive away...

I've thought about this for a long time and the conclusion is simple: motor dealerships and the salespeople who sell you your dream car are missing a trick, or dare I say three. The experience certainly isn't broken, but it is without a doubt stagnant. Look under the bonnet, in the boot or in the glove box... but where is the Secret Sauce?

When your competitors are doing pretty much the same and you all follow the industry norm, the rut is slowly formed, and it's not so easy to get out of it. It just takes one person to stand up and say, 'Can we create a better experience here?'

In truth, we don't have time to wait for them to stand up, and that's OK, as we can create our very own competitive advantage right here, right now, with the help of this next 120 Challenge.

It's time to re-imagine this experience. It's time to assemble your pit lane crew, your team, your colleagues, and let us spark this experience into life as if we were the motor dealership on handover day.

120 CHALLENGE

QUESTION 1: What could you do for the customer to create a greater Celebrity Service experience when taking the order? Remember, it could be months or up to a year before their car arrives.

QUESTION 2: What could you do for the customer in the months or weeks in the build-up to handover day?

QUESTION 3: The big day has arrived – handover day is here!!! What could you do for the customer to create an experience that will live long in their memory?

Good luck.

WHAT WOULD YOU DO, GEOFF?

If I were to own a motor dealership, these are the three Secret Sauce toppings I'd put in place to create differentiation with my competitors...

Idea 1

There is a good chance you will have to wait months and potentially up to a year for your car to be built, shipped and ready to drive. During conversations with the customer, I wouldn't just give them a receipt, brochure or a printout of their car order. I'd ensure they took away the car right there and then! I'd simply shrink the model they had just ordered to a toy version. This would work even better if a family arrived in the showroom with younger children. This would be their little gift for coming along with their parents, and it would cost just a couple of pounds, dollars or euros at most. The conversation would flow as follows:

'So, your mum and dad have just bought their brand new car,

and it's so big it's going to take a while to build it in the factory. However, would you like your very own version of the car they have chosen? Let's see if our workshop has made one just for you…'

You leave your desk.

A few minutes later, you walk back into the room and approach the child with the toy car (the exact model and colour of the one purchased), wrapped up and in a branded bag or box, and say, 'Here is your very own car. Now, keep this by your bedside and remember to bring it with you when your mum and dad next visit…'

I wonder how much the child would smile? I wonder what the parents (customers) would be thinking in that moment? I wonder if they would capture an image of the model car and their child that would create more traction on social media than any of the dealer's advertisements?

Of course, what this needs is a buy-in from the team and someone to source hundreds of tiny cars to keep in stock. But that's the easy part. The hard part has already been done – and now the idea is yours (if you are a motor dealer reading this book).

The tiny toy car becomes your Secret Sauce.

Idea 2

If there is a long to-do list, then help is on its way – with a planner, complete with accurate timeline, useful numbers, website links – a proper step-by-step guide to the whole process.

This could be sent to the customer as an app from the dealership, as an email attachment or a printed out version to stick on your fridge or put on your desk.

With a month to go, this is what you need to do next…

When you have received this, now do this…. (include links).

Click here to get your....

Not everyone is a seasoned car buying and selling expert, so the minefield I described at the beginning of this section could all be navigated more easily if the dealer gave the customer this in advance to avoid any last-minute surprises or delays. Sounds obvious, doesn't it? But this can work in any business or sector – a financial professional could offer the same timeline planner for tax, VAT deadlines, dividends, etc.

The planner becomes your Secret Sauce.

Idea 3

Apart from activating the 'new car smell', there are more senses you could awaken as the car is about to be unveiled.

So let's add some visuals and sounds. I'd darken the room completely (maybe add some low-level floor lights like the ones you see on planes). I'd also introduce spotlights that would point towards the vehicle. These would be switched on when everyone was ready. To add to the effect, I'd add some subtle music (no radio channels with adverts allowed here). If you've ever queued for a thrill ride at a theme park, there are sights and sounds that create excitement, tension and suspense – so why not for this industry? Creating a sense of Disney or Lucasfilm-style theatre would have you talked about and recommended for years to come.

The theatre becomes your Secret Sauce.

There you go – three ideas to reignite a stagnant customer experience. What did you or your team come up with? Who became the Celebrity Service superstars of this interactive challenge?

A few things to remember...

I'm sure the car handover that Hollywood actors like Chris Hemsworth or Jennifer Lawrence receive is a little different to the one you or I, aka 'the normal customer', receives. It's all about discovering the gap in your service you never knew existed and delivering the Secret Sauce consistently each and every time.

And for every great idea, there will always be a bump in the road to halt your progress from actioning the idea. After all, it's easy to come up with excuses, such as where would we store all the toy cars? Who will update the planner? How will we get the lights and sounds to work together?

But this is about differentiating your service experience, going beyond that of your competitors and, dare I say, becoming famous for the experience you deliver.

Anyone can sell cars. Not everyone can deliver the experience.

Oh, and would I reintroduce flowers? Why not? No one else is doing it.

Welcome to EXPERIENCE MAKERS

Welcome to the most exciting, interactive and rewarding experience for you and your colleagues in creating and maintaining service excellence.

With every Experience Makers challenge, your team will generate the most amazing customer service experiences.

Unlike the 120 Challenges, which are a sure-fire way to boost ideas in just two minutes, Experience Makers is a longer, more detailed challenge from my Celebrity Service keynotes and programmes.

WHAT'S THE AIM OF EXPERIENCE MAKERS?

For your teams to work together to create greater service experience ideas and strategies.

HOW LONG WILL IT TAKE?

It could take as little as one day, a week or even a full month (depending on your schedule). Please note, if you go for a month, make sure to send reminders so that everyone is focused on service excellence ideas.

HOW MANY CAN TAKE PART?

From two to two million! Any number of teams in any organisation can take part and contribute. You set the number.

HOW DO YOU DELIVER THE CHALLENGE?

You can do this via a group meeting or an internal email (if your teams are spread across different locations or time zones) or, better still, record yourself reading out the challenge on a video and send it to your teams. PS: you must set a deadline for the challenge to end – for example, no later than 15:58 on Tuesday 11 March.

WHAT KIND OF IDEAS ARE YOU LOOKING FOR?

You are really after the Secret Sauce (the one thing that will deliver a better customer experience). Inform your teams that they can go big and spend a fortune, or be clever with a shoestring budget. What you want them to achieve is a list of ideas that they can use straight away, adapt for tomorrow or save for a rainy day.

WHAT HAPPENS WHEN THE RESULTS START ARRIVING?

Collect all the entries and store them in a dedicated Experience Makers folder. When the deadline passes, you can now watch or read them and pick out a shortlist of the very best, most imaginative and maybe one or two of the craziest ideas.

WHO WINS?

The winners are those who have come up with the best service ideas and concepts. It could be something you tweak to make it easier for the customer. It could be something that would be cost-effective and simple to create. You choose who should win, but if it's too close to call, put it to a team vote.

WHAT'S NEXT?

Once the winner or winners have been chosen, it's time to 'feed forward' the ideas from the challenge. Ideally, you would record a video thanking everyone for taking part, then reveal the very best ideas. Share why they were chosen and then congratulate them by awarding them a prize.

WHAT DO THEY WIN?

Again, this is completely up to you, but here are a few ideas: a day off work, pizzas this Friday for the winning team or a big box of chocolate/candy.

WHAT WOULD YOU DO, GEOFF?

Personally, I'd award the team a certificate for the wall – it would be printed, framed and mounted for everyone to see.

Please remember that this should be seen as a fun and creative competition that encourages everyone to contribute, develop and see what real Celebrity Service in your organisation could look like.

SHARING THE IDEAS

All of the answers received should also be collected and shared with your teams and departments. You never know, one idea could spark off another in a different department, which leads to an even better idea.

Without further ado, are you order takers or experience makers?

Are you and your team up for the challenge?

Will you become true Experience Makers?

Let's create some Secret Sauce for the Celebrity Service experience...

EXPERIENCE MAKERS:
ALL FOUR ONE

The Experience Makers concept was born from a question I was asked on social media.

QUESTION: Geoff – any ideas on how to deliver a great internal experience to any of our team?

As I got into a conversation online, it transpired that the client was asking for specific ideas to reward a rather loyal member of the team who had been with the business for more than two decades.

I said I'd think about it and, later that week, came back with four ideas they could use or adapt. However, as budgets hadn't been mentioned, I took the decision to create four ideas for this one person using different amounts of investment. And so, All Four One was created.

Watch the video and share it with your team, as I'm sure they will all become Experience Makers for one of their own colleagues one day.

Chapter 1
BELTING IDEAS

AIRPORT ADVENTURES

You can spend hours mooching around an airport terminal, browsing the stores and visiting a restaurant or bar.

Then you spend time at the gate before being ushered onto a bus to drive you to your plane, more often than not to the furthest point imaginable on the runway.

You then spend ages (sometimes more than a full day) flying to your destination.

But in all of this experience, waiting for your luggage to arrive on the carousel can seem like the longest wait of all. It's this last touchpoint that is stopping you from continuing your onward journey.

It's crucial to position your body near the conveyor belt for a quick grab 'n' get away, but which way will the belt go? Will you have to adjust when the orange light begins to flash? And this is all tinged with anxiety as you wonder, 'Did my case actually make it?'

What will usually take around 15 minutes to arrive seems an eternity compared with the time you've already endured. So, what would you do to make this a better experience while you wait?

At Madrid airport, they have installed dozens of television screens (four per carousel). While we were waiting, two of the screens were showing

CELEBRITY SERVICE SECRET SAUCE

a live tennis match from the Madrid Open and the other two were showing children's cartoons. If your bags take longer than expected (ours certainly did), then at least you are distracted and entertained, making this a better experience for travellers.

At Newcastle airport, following your inbound Jet2 flight, the very first case to arrive on the belt will never be yours! Even if your case is taken out of the cargo hold first, it simply will not be yours. Instead, you will see a bright red case and, strangely enough, there is nothing inside.

Jet2 delivers a lovely piece of Celebrity Service by having the baggage handlers place their Jet2 case on the belt well before any other cases. This way, everyone gathered around will see the Jet2 brand and their final message to you…

At any point in the experience when your customers have to wait, what can you do to distract, engage or even say 'thank you' to them?

120

120 Challenge
HAPPY TO BE DELAYED

120 CHALLENGE

120

Ahh – airport lounges. Those havens of relaxation, chilled beverages, fresh food, plus multiple screens informing you about your flight, gate number and how long it will take you to walk there. And then there's the most important thing in the world today – sockets to charge your electronics.

Like anything in business, they differ slightly from airport to airport, airline to airline and country to country but, let's face it, 99 per cent of them are all fairly similar.

But what if you and your team owned your own airport lounge? Would you settle for providing the same as everyone else? Or would you set about creating an amazing experience – so amazing, in fact, that if the flight were delayed, the passengers would actually be happy!?

This next 120 Challenge is a very simple one.

What would you put in your lounge area to make this the most talked-about in the world today?

You can go crazy on the budget if you like, or be as frugal as can be while still delivering a great experience for the passenger. The choice is yours.

Good luck.

WHAT HAVE YOU SEEN, GEOFF?

On my travels, I've been fortunate enough to see inside one or two airport lounges. Some are lovely, while others need a lot of tender, loving care. Some are sparse, and many are overcrowded. But there is one that stands out head rest and shoulders above them all – Muscat airport in Oman.

In what sounds like The Twelve Days of Christmas, this is what I observed. There were two full-size pool tables, giant TV screens, Foosball tables, a seated football game, and a room full of toys for smaller children, with another television showing cartoons. Oh, and there was also a family cinema room.

I played pool for over an hour, and when my flight was called, I can't deny that I was disappointed.

What did you and your teams come up with? I would love to hear your ideas.

Chapter 2
THREE CAME ALONG AT ONCE

A TALE OF THREE TAXIS

Any taxi driver can drive you from A to B, but what sets them apart is the Secret Sauce they apply at any stage of the journey. It can start before you get into the vehicle, to the first ten seconds of your trip, and through to pulling up at your destination.

Here's a trio of drivers who went from A to B to Celebrity…

THIS IS THE LIFT YOU'VE BEEN LOOKING FOR…

After collecting my case from the carousel at Southampton Airport (sadly, there are no televisions to be found here), I walked through the automatic doors into the arrivals area, where my next travel challenge was to look for the taxi driver who was waiting for me.

It always feels a little weird having to walk gingerly along a line of drivers who are each holding a small card or screen, trying to spot your name. What if you get to the end of the line and you can't see your name? Do you do the whole reverse-back-in-shame walk? Is your driver there at all?

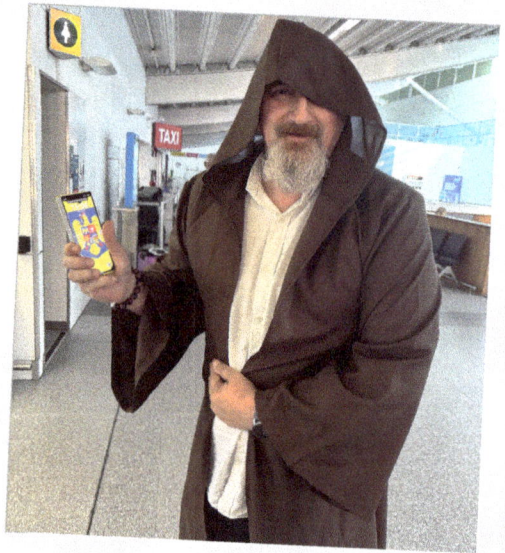

I needn't have worried, as I think I may have spotted the driver in the arrivals docking bay.

My friend and client Douglas Taylor, vice president of guest experience at P&O Cruises, shares the same passion as I do for Star Wars, so he tasked his team with creating a welcome I would never forget.

The team contacted a local taxi company and a wonderful gentleman called Stefan (also a big fan of Star Wars) purchased a couple of Jedi robes (as he wasn't sure of the correct size), got dressed and entered the airport.

He met me with the following greeting: 'Welcome, Master, to Hampshire. Let me take your bags.'

When you know something about your customer, take the opportunity to use that information to deliver an unforgettable Secret Sauce experience.

When it comes to taxi drivers, there seems to be something in the Floridian air. First, there was Uber Nick and the wonderful ways in which he pre-empted what his passengers would like or need (you may remember him from the first Celebrity Service book). And now we have two more Celebrity Service superstars, who poured some Secret Sauce over a short trip.

A MUSICAL MARVEL

The Uber was booked. Our driver was called Sean and this time our final destination was Epcot.

On our journey to the theme park, we spoke about the rides and attractions and in which order we were hopefully going to get on them via the Disney FastPass (which is a military operation in itself).

As we drove, Sean asked us what our number one must-see attraction would be at Epcot. And we all answered with the same four words: Guardians of the Galaxy.

We pulled off the highway and drove through the main entrance to Epcot. At this precise moment, Sean reached over to the music collection on his dashboard and selected the next song – which just happened to be the Avengers soundtrack that features the Guardians of the Galaxy!!!

I often go to bed wondering if Sean is in any way related to Eric, who works at Madison Square Garden (you'll meet Eric on page 72)? I may never know.

It was an unexpected experience that deserves to be highlighted and recognised, but before we leave the vehicle, there is someone very special I want to introduce you to and put on a Secret Sauce pedestal…

THE BIGGEST TIP OF ALL

Imagine for one moment jumping into a taxi and within ten seconds all you want to do is give the driver the biggest tip and the highest rating on the Uber app.

What on Earth would have to happen to make you want to do this?

What would the driver have said to you?

How about the vehicle – was it a Porsche, a Ferrari or a monster truck (this is Florida, after all)?

The answer is the reason why Dianna drives a taxi.

I was sitting in the front and we all exchanged pleasantries and the usual tourist Q&A.

Where are you from?

When did you arrive?

What are you looking forward to most?

Have you been to England?

That sort of thing.

After ten seconds, Hayley tapped me on the shoulder and as I looked round, she was pointing at a note attached to the back of Dianna's seat.

Here's a photo of the note so you can see what it said...

ive for charity. Everything I earn through Uber I donate to a different charity
ch month. So far I have donated over $6000.00 from June 2021 to current.
e charities I've donated to do far are: American Cancer Society, March of
nes, Give the Kids the World, Diabetes Foundation, Heath Project for
meless children in schools, Lakeland Homeless Coalition, Lighthouse
nistries, Polk County Children's Home, Food banks, Toys for Tots and next
onth will A.L.S. Foundation. If there's a charity near & dear to your heart ✿ ✿,
ease let me know and I'll donate to that as well. By choosing me you're
elping me help others. So thank you.

Tips greatly appreciated. ☺
Thank you!

We all thought this was amazing, and it became a real talking point.
So, for the duration of the journey, we chatted about Dianna's
chosen charities.

Dianna has retired but still wants to help and support her local
community. And as we were in one of the world's busiest tourist
hotspots, she took the opportunity to meet new people and raise
funds to support local charities by driving them around the Disney
and Universal parks.

We live in a world where we can promote our charitable work,
use our connections and social influence to leverage support,
donations and awareness. However, what made this extra
special Secret Sauce was that it was unexpected and very much
understated – just a simple message and a 'thank you' printed on a
piece of paper for anyone to read and potentially help the charities.

EXPERIENCE MAKERS: FIRST DAY, LASTING IMPRESSION

We often believe that customer service is for the guest, client, passenger or member. However, as I have always said, just like charity, Celebrity Service starts at home. It starts with you, your team, your colleagues, your department, your business, your organisation.

Set the foundations of a great, happy and inspired team and this culture will rub off onto your customers.

We've all been through this experience: your very first day at work. You probably didn't sleep all that well the night before; you may have bought some new shoes, pens and pencils (similar to your first day at school) and you will naturally feel a little nervous. You'd set your alarm earlier than usual as you didn't want to be late on your first day. It's a big time in your life.

But what sort of experience did you have on your very first day at your current place of work? Did you walk through the door thinking, 'Wow, I've made the best decision to move'? There are dozens of touchpoints that can create the Secret Sauce to your onboarding experience.

- Were they expecting you?
- How long did you have to wait to meet someone?
- What did they say?
- Who did you meet?
- Where did you eat?
- Was everything ready for you?
- Was your desk ready?
- Was your desktop or laptop fully charged and raring to go?
- Were your passwords complete?

- Were your business cards (if you had them) already printed?
- Overall, how was the experience?

Was it so amazing you couldn't wait to shout from the rooftops that night? Was it so amazing you took to social media to share those experiences? Or was it similar to everywhere else you've ever worked?

Maybe it was a Celebrity Service experience or maybe it was a forgettable experience.

The reality may have been something like the following. You arrive, and they don't know who you are at the front desk. No one has set up an email for you, and passwords will take another week to come through. You have to use a guest log-in instead. Maybe you waited more than three weeks for your business cards, which is funny, given that your team had known you were coming for months!

If you were Bradley Cooper or Priyanka Chopra, I bet your very first day would look and feel slightly different.

But fear not – the greatest ever day your future colleague is about to experience is just around the corner, thanks to Celebrity Service Experience Makers and finding your 'onboarding Secret Sauce'.

You have the opportunity to create something truly memorable for your next colleague.

- What could you send your new colleague one week before they arrive, so they are excited and can't wait to join you?
- When they walk through the door or if they are working remotely, what are they met with, what do they get, what do they see?

I want them to think that THIS is the greatest place they have ever worked!

Chapter 3
ALWAYS MAKING YOU SMILE

THE POWER OF A LITTLE EXTRA

My earliest recollections of seeing a professional comedian go way back to the Rainbow Hotel in Torquay, when I was still in short trousers on a family holiday. In the ballroom that evening was none other than *Runaround*'s very own Mike Reid. I can't remember a single joke, but I do remember I loved it.

From listening to the albums of the godfather of comedy, Billy Connolly, to seeing him perform live, from Ricky Gervais and Jim Jefferies (have you watched or listened to the 'Downgraded' story yet?) to Rob Brydon and Clinton Baptiste, I just love watching comedians and their sheer storytelling brilliance, unfolding into a perfect punchline.

'But what has this got to do with Celebrity Service Secret Sauce, Geoff?' I hear you ask. Well, there are two wonderful examples of what two of my favourites do right after their show to add to the experience.

First, my fellow sand dancer, Sarah Millican (sand dancer is the colloquial term for someone born in South Shields). Other notable people from South Shields include Dame Catherine Cookson, Eric Idle of Monty Python fame, Sir Ridley Scott, Sir Frank Williams and, of course, Perrie Edwards and Jade Thirlwall from Little Mix (Grace would not be happy if I omitted these two from the list!).

In every one of Sarah's shows, she lets the audience know before her finale that she has a gift for everyone as they leave the theatre. The gift is a small pin badge that features a word, a phrase or a saying from the show that becomes a souvenir of your night. We have seen her four times now and each time we take a badge away with us. It's small, it's inexpensive, but it's a lovely little 'thank you' gift from a famous comedian, which enhances the experience of the night.

Gift your customer a 'money can't buy' token of your appreciation. That's Secret Sauce.

Storytelling is such an art form, and a well-crafted one-liner can bring the house down. I am a huge fan of Mark Simmons. I'd watched a lot of his short videos on his social channels (go check them out). He's brilliant. I first saw him at the Consett Comedy Festival and, during the break, I walked up to the back of the room and, as luck would have it, Mark was there. I congratulated him on a great set, we shook hands and had a photo taken.

On the same night, we booked tickets to see him again only a few weeks later at the Gala Theatre in Durham, on his own UK tour.

On this occasion, he delivered his final joke, we cheered, we clapped, he walked off, we got up, we walked out of the theatre, and as luck would have it, he was in the foyer again. I congratulated him on his set, we shook hands, and as we hadn't really changed much in three weeks there was no need for a second photograph.

As we left the theatre, it dawned on me.

He does this at every gig. He finishes his set, he hurriedly walks off stage and out into the foyer to shake hands with everyone who attended and say, 'Thank you for coming.'

To take the time to thank people and have your photograph taken with them shows a huge amount of respect for your current and future fans.

It sounds obvious, but show your customers you appreciate them. That's Secret Sauce.

ECOSSE EXCELLENCE

Scotland is blessed with many great writers, from Arthur Conan Doyle to Alistair MacLean, but I have two more wonderful examples to add that show how putting words on paper or indeed onto a screen will help transform the experience for the reader…

MAYA JUST SAYS THANKS…

I was booked to deliver a keynote speech in Glasgow for the Association of Scotland's Self-Caterers. It was a wonderful event and, right after my talk, one of the delegates, Maya Rarity, came up to me and enthusiastically thanked me for my ideas, stories and inspiration. She told me she was now following me on social media and, later that day as I was travelling back on the train, she tagged me in her posts. We exchanged pleasantries, connected and stayed in touch.

When you connect with someone or their business, you'll often click and scroll to find out a little more about what they do. I discovered that Maya has two fabulous holiday apartments in Edinburgh.

I started to scroll her profile on X and my eyebrows started to raise at the type of posts I was viewing. I'd never seen anything like them before.

After EVERY guest had stayed at the holiday apartment, Maya would take to X and personally thank each and every one of them.

Best of all, she doesn't know the guests' social media addresses, but despite not having this crucial information, she still takes the time to thank all of them.

Right now, you've probably put down the book to take a look for yourself, so let me help with a quick shortcut – go to @RarityBreaks on X.

If you don't want to put the book down, I have highlighted a selection of these posts…

You'll know the sayings, 'Dance like no one is watching' and, 'Sing like no one is listening'. Well, maybe in the world of Celebrity Service, the Secret Sauce version is, 'Appreciate when no one is reading'.

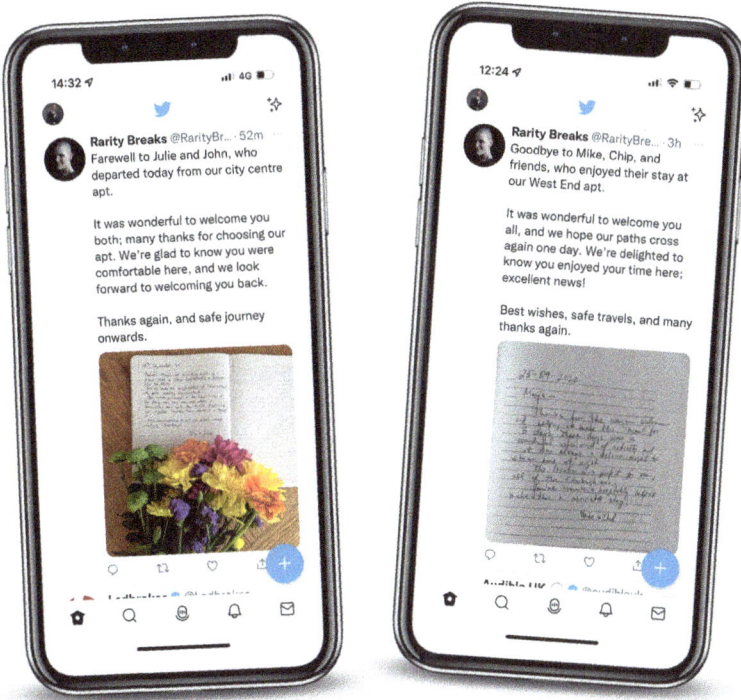

WRITTEN TEST – A*

Despite my background in the world of business, I work a lot in education – whether it's head teacher conferences, working on inset days with the staff, or lectures at private, public and boarding schools, from primary and secondary to colleges and universities.

When a client books me, I will of, course, research their online and social profiles to gain an understanding of their language, which helps me to create the talk just for them.

On the odd occasion, I may also make contact – not as a mystery shopper, but as someone wanting to understand how things work, what is said, what is sent, etc.

One of the greatest examples was my experience with Strathallan School in Perthshire. The date had been set and the briefing call had concluded. But before I drove up through the Scottish borders, I made an enquiry about our son, Elliot, via the website.

The system asked various questions about his hobbies and interests, and I filled it all in to see what might happen. (The school had no idea it was me, nor that I would be speaking there in a month's time.)

I filled out the form and pressed send, asking for a prospectus to be posted to me.

It arrived two days later in a wonderful thick, dark blue envelope! The prospectus oozed quality and gave you the feel of a school that would be a great place to learn and excel. Elliot did notice it on my desk and genuinely thought he was being moved to another country. I had to tell him it was part of my work.

Inside the prospectus was a covering letter. And this is when the Secret Sauce moment arrived...

On the left-hand side of the letter was a QR code, nestled on top of the Millennium Falcon. Did they know? How could they know?

It was addressed 'Dear Elliot' and the greatest paragraph is what you are about to read:

Follow in the footsteps of Olympians with our exceptional sporting facilities and take your football skills to the next level. Thanks to our floodlit astroturf pitches and indoor multi-sports hall, whatever the weather you can play football all year round at Strathallan, just like at the Stadium of Light.

They must have researched my socials! And, of course, they took note of Elliot's interest in football and the fact that we live just a mile from the Stadium of Light, home to Sunderland FC.

If I were marking this paper, I'd write a huge 'SEE ME' in red ink on the bottom – and when the team came to see me, I'd congratulate them on creating one of the best letters I have ever seen.

Chapter 4
WHEN THE STARS COME OUT...

IT'S SHOWTIME...

You can either ignore the world around you or embrace it to increase the experience for your customers. One costs nothing and the experience stays the same. The other takes effort, but the rewards will mean you're remembered and hopefully rebooked in future.

The choice is yours. Choose well.

Here are two that embraced it (but you can change that).

READY FOR IT?

When the dates were announced for Taylor Swift's Eras tour, the scramble for tickets was insane, to say the least. And even if you were successful, you still panicked, knowing you had to quickly reserve train tickets and, as the concert would go on into the night, book accommodation as well.

Booking a room for our daughter Grace and her friend was harder than obtaining Taylor's tickets! With half a year to go, every availability via various websites had vanished into thin air. Edinburgh is a beautiful place and always packed with tourists, but every room taken? Everywhere was full? It's as if... oh, hang on...

Let's just say I was never top of the class when it came to fully understanding supply and demand economics. If only the lecturer would have said, 'If the world's biggest music star came to your city, all prices would increase,' I would have got a better grade!

After a week or so, a few rooms did become available but the price made this into a cruel summer, for sure. Continuous searching ensued, until we found a Staycity Aparthotel. Perfect! I have worked for and stayed in the serviced apartment sector and their product is brilliant! The price was 'normal' too. We booked.

On the day of the concert, Grace arrived at the property and within minutes my WhatsApp lit up.

'Look at this, Dad. Look at what they have done.'

To welcome their guests, the team at Staycity had decorated their foyer. They chose well.

A GOLDEN TRIOMPHE

In the summer of 2024, the Olympic Games were held in Paris. As luck would have it, I was booked to speak in Paris just as the Paralympics were about to start. My client booked me into the Renaissance hotel just a five-minute walk from the Arc de Triomphe.

As I arrived, I didn't know whether to walk, run or sprint, as they had created a running track that took you to the main entrance. Above my head, there were gold medals hanging from the ceiling. In the reception area they had a podium for guests to stand on and take photographs. There was a dressing table full of make-up and paints so guests could decorate their faces to show their support for their nation. And along the mirrored back wall of the breakfast bar, the team had hand-drawn every nation's flag to welcome every nationality.

Chapter 5
DOING IT FOR THE KIDS

BRIDGING THE GAP

Whether he's playing for his club, his school, on his PlayStation or watching Sunderland with me, his sister Grace and his mum Hayley, my son, Elliot, loves his football.

So, on a family trip to London, the girls had gone to see Mamma Mia! The Party while Elliot and I had a few hours spare in the morning. So what could the boys do? Where could we go?

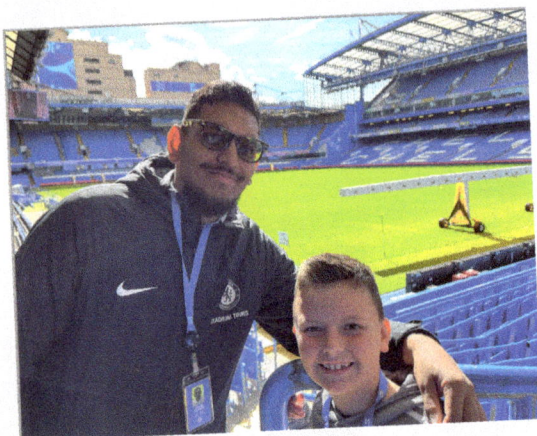

Ideally, I wanted to get up close to a football club I know Elliot would have seen many times on his video games and on television. We were too far from Arsenal and Tottenham Hotspur and I wasn't sure he'd appreciate a trip to Queen's Park Rangers, so we jumped in a taxi and headed to Stamford Bridge, home of Chelsea Football Club. All I wanted to do was show him the stadium, have a walk around, take a picture or two and maybe pop into their club shop (if it was open on a Sunday).

We arrived, the sun was shining on SW6 and photographs were taken, so we started to walk around the outside of the stadium. As luck would have it, the museum was open, along with the stadium tours. We didn't have time for the tour, so briskly took in the museum. Elliot was in his element looking at the trophies and strips, as well as playing football in their interactive area. I must admit I was in my element too, looking at the old Panini sticker albums. I also viewed the 1980s Chelsea strip sponsored by Commodore 64, which I had when I was Elliot's age.

Anyhow, back to the real Secret Sauce of Stamford Bridge. The photographer who took our picture next to the Champions League trophy was superb. The guide, I think his name was George, was so helpful in the museum. And then there was Eklim Rahman, who really put in a captain's performance.

When we were at the till collecting our Champions League photograph and were just about to leave the museum, Eklim walked over to us and asked if we were going on the tour. We said we'd have loved to, but sadly we didn't have time. He leaned in and whispered, 'Follow me, let's see if we can get you into the ground so you can take a quick picture.'

It's a sentence and an experience Elliot will never forget.

We walked across the road, Eklim brought out his janitor-esque set of keys, opened the gate and we entered the stadium. We walked through the concourse and stepped out into the Matthew Harding Stand. Elliot couldn't stop smiling. It was something so simple that once again cost nothing but made a great experience even greater.

This book is full of these little touches, those tiny moments that heighten the service experience. However, not everyone does this. Not everyone spots the opportunity and takes action. Because it's not as simple as I am making out here.

Let's rewind a little, as to make moments like this happen, Eklim must do a few things for Elliot to receive an amazing Celebrity Service:

He must be near enough to a customer to engage with them.

He needs to make the decision to speak to the customer. (Some might, most won't.)

Once he asks a question, he needs to listen closely to the response.

Armed with the customer's answer, it is now down to him to say or do something to elevate their experience.

The funniest part of the weekend happened just after we left the ground, when Elliot turned to me and said, 'Is he going to be in your next book, Dad? Are you going to talk about him on stage?'

'Maybe, Elliot, just maybe…'

WHEN HARRY MET…

There are three guarantees in life: death, taxes and, should a single note of a One Direction song be played in a hotel foyer, supermarket or anywhere for that matter, our daughter, Grace, will stop whatever she's doing, leap up and, with a huge smile on her face, start singing every single word of that song!

From day one, she has been one of those 1D superfans. Not just the band, but after they split, she became a fan of their solo journeys – especially multi-award-winning artist and Hollywood actor, Harry Styles.

As a family, we entered the legendary Madison Square Garden. Grace had great pleasure in telling me that Harry had recently set a record of 15 consecutive 'sold out' nights at the New York City arena. In fact, Mr Styles' ticket sales were phenomenal, with more than 277,000 sold, grossing over $63 million (according to Billboard magazine). Not only did he become the biggest UK artist to play there, he also became the biggest male artist to play there, and indeed the biggest selling act to play there in the iconic venue's history.

Our tour of the arena began.

Our guide for the next hour was a charismatic, knowledgeable gentleman by the name of Eric, who liked to crack a joke. He pointed out the history of the venue with some of its most iconic moments from basketball, hockey and boxing. He also spoke at length about the famous 'Happy birthday, Mr President' performance by Marilyn Monroe.

Halfway through the tour, we arrived at the corporate boxes. We took our plush seats and I happened to look up and notice a flag hanging from the ceiling. I nudged Grace and her eyes lit up. The flag read: 'HARRY STYLES 15 CONSECUTIVE NIGHTS AT THE GARDEN'.

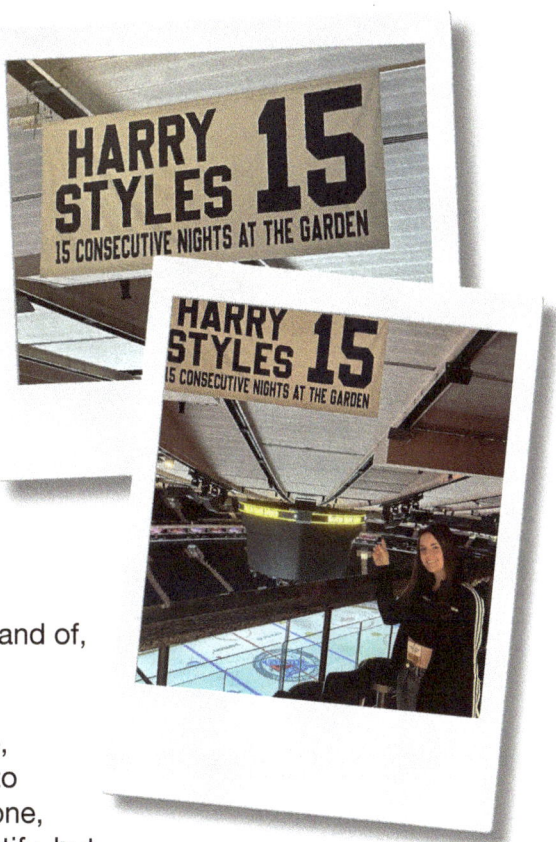

Eric spotted this and asked if Grace was a Harry Styles fan.

The blue touchpaper had been lit.

We left the boxes to take the escalator up to the top level (and of, course, nearer the flag).

As we entered the concourse, I noticed Eric had reached into his pocket, pulled out his phone, opened an app (possibly Spotify, but other streaming services are available) and played a track, so that when everyone was walking through, 'As It Was' by none other than Harry Styles was playing loudly on his phone…

This simple act of thought and kindness made our daughter's day. Eric reduced the volume and proceeded to talk about the record-breaking artist in depth before photographs were taken.

This would have been a good tour.

But with a great tour guide, it became memorable.

Eric spotted an opportunity and took it, which made this a great experience.

The Secret Sauce is often the thing that costs nothing but means the world to someone.

Eric, we Adore You!

120

120 Challenge
I WANT LOVE

The news breaks: one of the world's greatest musicians has just released their global tour dates, and it just happens to be their final tour.

You check to see where they will be playing and when.

As luck would have it, they are coming to a stadium that just happens to be one mile from where you live.

At 8 am, you proceed to open three laptops, two tablets, one desktop and a smartphone as you begin the wonderful journey of queuing online for tickets. The message flashes across all your devices: 'Congratulations, you are only number 17.4 million in the queue, we'll be with you shortly.'

Second mortgage approved (to cover the cost of printing your tickets at home, using your own paper and ink… I know, I promise I'm not going to go there on this occasion) and, just like that, your tickets have been purchased.

Sir Elton Hercules John – we are coming to see your Farewell Yellow Brick Road tour.

Coldplay, Beyonce, Bruce Springsteen, Oasis and Ed Sheeran have all been played in Sunderland and, as you can imagine, concerts of this size bring with them great footfall and investment into the area.

So imagine if you will, owning a restaurant only a short walk away from the stadium. You've had months to plan for this big occasion. Forty-five thousand tickets have been sold, and you have steadily taken bookings from locals and travelling fans alike. You are now fully booked for the day. This is a big opportunity to remind local customers of what you offer as well as impressing customers from outside the area so they will want to return.

This is a golden opportunity for you to deliver Celebrity Service…

120 CHALLENGE

Let's create some Secret Sauce for the customers at your restaurant with the 'I Want Love' Celebrity Service 120 Challenge…

QUESTION 1: What could you do to create an experience everyone will talk about for years to come? To give you and your team a head start, think of the following:

The wording on the email or text that you send out to confirm your restaurant reservation.

What could your staff be wearing? Make a list.

Could you tweak the menu choices in some way to reflect this big event?

Think about the ambience – what could you hear in the background as you are enjoying your meal?

Your two minutes to generate amazing experiences has just started.

Good luck.

As you know by now, this is not a made-up challenge. Everything I deliver on stage or write about on these pages is based on true, real-life examples and experiences.

My wife Hayley and I and our good friends Martin and Jude visited a local restaurant before Elton took to the stage.

We booked, we arrived, we ate, we drank, we laughed, we left. And to be honest with you, apart from the company, nothing about our visit was memorable.

The food was 5/10 at best, but the overall experience would be around 4/10. It was fine. But in a competitive world where your customers have many choices, it could have been so much better.

Everyone in that restaurant was heading to the same place to see the same person, but sadly zero effort was made, and therefore the experience was forgettable.

When the waiter came over to take our credit cards, I couldn't hold back and chirped up with my first idea: 'I thought you'd all be wearing huge Elton John glasses to get into the spirit of things.' He looked at me blankly.

Undeterred, I continued with my second idea: 'You know, if you had played all his hit songs through your speakers, it would have got everyone in the mood. I reckon we'd have all joined in with some singing.'

He looked at me with a 'Cold Heart' and said: 'Nah, they're not bothered.'

Now, what I should have asked was, 'Who wasn't bothered? The customers or the owners of the restaurant?'

Either way, it wouldn't have been a great 'Sacrifice' to create something memorable, and sadly another opportunity to deliver a Celebrity Service experience was lost.

Incidentally, if Reggie Dwight had booked, there may just have been a bit more thought and effort made... maybe.

WHAT WOULD YOU DO, GEOFF?

It's very simple, really. I'd buy 100 pairs of huge, colourful, fun sunglasses (I might have invested a little more and had the name of the restaurant printed on the side as a souvenir). These would be given to every customer, and if they wore them for the duration of their meal, they would win a prize and receive a free, Elton-inspired drink.

Imagine the number of selfies and posts these would have helped to generate, both inside the restaurant and the stadium? It may have had future music lovers checking out this restaurant before the next event, knowing that they love to create a fabulous experience.

I would have had great fun creating a special menu, with names of the dishes twisted to sound like Elton albums, lyrics or songs. Apologies for the incoming cheesiness...

- Can You Feel the Loaf Tonight?
- I'm Dill Standing.
- Don't Go Breaking My a la Carte.
- Chocodile Rock.
- Goodbye Yellow Brick Rocky Road.

You could even have fun with the conversations between the staff and customers: 'How would you like your eggs? It's a little bit runny...'

Hire an Elton John lookalike to sign and pose for photos around the tables.

Hire a local singer to sing his hits.

And, of course, the easiest one of them all – just press bloomin' PLAY on your Sir Elton John playlist.

Overall, it was a great night, but we have yet to return to the restaurant.

If you truly want repeat business, then please think about an experience that will entice people back.

It's not 'Rocket Man' science.

So how did your 120 Challenge go? What did you and your teams create?

Chapter 6
RATHER
EVENTFUL

EVENTS WITH A TWIST

If there's one industry I know more about than most, it's the one I work in – the high-pressured, often bonkers yet hugely inspirational world of events and conferences.

I have a huge amount of respect for event planners who design, create and deliver for their audiences, whether it be smaller internal company events or global, multi-day conferences.

From choosing venues to selecting menus, picking themes and booking AV teams, creating a successful conference is just like organising a wedding (and many of us know how stress-free that is!).

There are the lanyards to print, maps to share, offsite trips to arrange, travel itineraries for planes, trains and automobiles, gala awards evenings, trophies to engrave, entertainment to hire, red carpets to lay and Fox's glacier mints to be placed right in the centre of the tables (other mint brands are available).

With so much to think about, the added Secret Sauce in creating memorable experiences is not an easy ask. To accomplish this, you must think a little differently to the rest, while looking to introduce a slice of personalisation that is unexpected for the delegates and indeed the speakers.

With this in mind, here are some of my favourites to help inspire you and your next event.

BUILT ON PERSONALISATION...

A plane was departing from Leeds Bradford airport to take many of the delegates to Portugal for the conference organised by building supplies firm MKM.

Every member of the team knew exactly which check-in desk they needed to go to, not because they were told beforehand, but because they could see their company logo proudly displayed on every screen.

I had flown through Newcastle airport to attend the event, so I did not see this. So how did I know? Well, at least half a dozen of the delegates came up to me right after my talk to show me the photos they had taken. They were amazed at what their company had done for them.

But it did not stop there, as there was another set of images they wanted to share. When they boarded the plane, the company logo was also printed and displayed on every headrest.

It was a great touch by the team at MKM and by the amazing First Event team who pulled all the creative ideas together.

HANG ON...

'A functional piece of plastic around your neck' is pretty much the best description of this event essential, but it's more than just your name badge. A lanyard featuring a logo or branding will inform venue staff and organisers which event you are a part of. It may well include an events itinerary on the back or a useful map for you to use.

However, at just about every event, they are all pretty much the same. That was until I attended and spoke at the Amaris (now Klarent Hospitality) conference in Glasgow.

The attendees were all hotel general managers, and when they collected their lanyard at the front desk, it had a large message on the front, followed by their digitally printed name, which completed the personalisation and made the recipient feel rather special.

A TEAM IN FINE TUNE

After a day-long conference comes the gala dinner/awards night, with great food, flowing wine and an air of excitement swirling around the room as to who will win an award or two.

I stayed at the same venue, the Hilton Doubletree in Glasgow, and things escalated to another level thanks to their management and kitchen team.

But what made it a night to remember?

Was it the Boogie Bingo that got everyone off their seats before the starters?

Was it the amazing group who played during our main course?

Was it the Darth Vader balloon and bottle of cider in my room to celebrate my 20th year in business? (This was a lovely touch from Klarent.)

Was it the printed magazine that was pushed under my bedroom door at 6 am featuring all the winning employees, their pictures and their stories from five hours earlier? (One of the best uses of digital print I have ever seen.)

It could have been any of those, but the Secret Sauce of this entire night was still to come. On the tables, the menu informed you of your starters and main course, but under desserts, all it said was: 'Played to piano'. The lights dimmed.

As the desserts were about to arrive, Coldplay's A Sky Full of Stars was played on the piano. Then, in came the waiters and waitresses, in unison, with the desserts... or should I say the showstoppers? The desserts were fully edible grand pianos made of chocolate, cream and fruit. All of the delegates and I were in awe.

Stewart Goldie was the head chef, and he and his team of three worked tirelessly for 35 days for this one big moment. General manager Craig Munro said: 'The inspiration for the dessert came from a Tom Lehrer quote, "Life is like a piano. What you get out of it depends on how you play it". We also decided to serve the desserts to the Coldplay hit as it represented people's dreams and aspirations.'

ACCOUNTING FOR TASTE

Have you ever wondered what was behind a lectern? It may come as no surprise to learn that it's normally a four-way extension lead, laptop, water, and sometimes the last speaker's notes.

AccountEX is a phenomenal conference that attracts thousands of financial professionals from the UK and around the world. It's the number one event in its sector, where companies and delegates showcase, promote, learn and network.

I was the opening speaker on their main stage at London's Excel venue. I arrived early to meet the tech team and run through my slide deck. For this particular talk, I had some props with me that I intended to use with the audience, so I hid them out of view behind the lectern:

- extension lead (check)
- laptop (check)
- water (check)
- notes from the last speaker (nope, as I was the first up)
- basket full of chocolate and sweets with a large note saying: 'SPEAKER ENERGY BOX' (check).

Wait, what???

Yes, that's right. Caroline Hobden and her team had put together a basket of treats just for the speakers, should they need an energy boost during their session!

I just about managed to get through the keynote without the need of a Boost, Twix or Milky Way, but couldn't help thinking this was a great Secret Sauce touch from the team.

MINI MADE ME!

The famous MADE: The Entrepreneur Festival in Sheffield was a dream to be a part of. There were only four of them, and I was fortunate enough to appear at three. They featured some amazing entrepreneurs, including Levi Roots of Reggae Reggae Sauce fame; Sahar Hashemi, founder of Coffee Republic and Steven Bartlett, who at the time was best known as the founder of Social Chain and one of the investors on Dragon's Den.

In the green room, there was a lovely touch in the fridge, as all the speakers had bottles of Coca-Cola with their names on them. Do you remember those?

There was a 'speaker survival pack' in our hotel bedrooms too, with useful, fun items for the event.

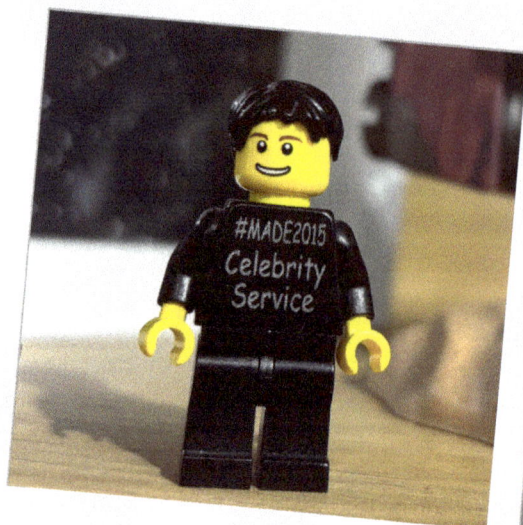

But, best of all, and the thing that is possibly still on our shelves today, was given our very own LEGO lookalike!!!

At the time, I had hair very similar to this. Thankfully, with one slight adjustment, I can still make it look like me today.

LIKE A GAME SHOW

My Celebrity Service interactive sessions create a huge buzz among teams. They're competitions that feature the 120 Challenges, which generate amazing ideas live in the room. And with every competition there must be winners. So, to recognise the teams that create the most creative, outlandish or brilliant ideas, we have to award them a prize.

Laura Coleby, CEO of marketing agency 67 Degrees, wanted to know which gifts they should get for our interactive session. On our briefing call, I jokingly said: 'Do you remember the TV game show, The Generation Game, where a conveyor belt of prizes would fill our screens?' And that was it. Laura went out and bought the sort of prizes you would have seen on the game show, including toasters, kettles and, of course, cuddly toys!!!

When I arrived at the venue, every prize was gift-wrapped, so the teams had no idea what was inside. This added to the experience and when the winning teams opened their gifts it became a mini Christmas morning.

FIRST PAST THE WINNING POST

These are not just cakes. These are M&T Hotel Management cakes.

Picture the scene... You're attending a day-long conference in Cheltenham (only a short trot from the racecourse). The morning break is called and you head towards the coffee station.

As you're filling your coffee cup, you notice that the Victoria sponge cakes have transformed into horses, with jockeys made from sugar paper on top, all set out on a table where they were racing up to the mini roll fences and the lemon drizzle obstacles!

This was such an 'exceedingly good' idea, with design, display and execution by Ben Sanders and his Doubletree hotel team, especially considering the pressure was on, as he had only been in the role for seven weeks and they were serving the general managers of the other M&T properties!

Everyone loved it. It was the talk of the conference.

WHERE TO GO? WHAT TO EAT?

At the conference in Rome for the global vehicle parts company LKQ, the team wanted to deliver a welcome gift into every delegate's bedroom – ideally, something useful, something memorable and, of course, something that showed you were in the Italian capital.

As I pulled my case into the bedroom, I could see a couple of gifts on the corner of my bed. The first was a guidebook and map of Rome, but the cover had been branded for the conference.

The other gift was a large bag of pasta with a wooden spoon attached. However, when you looked closely, you could see every pasta shape was, in fact, the LKQ logo! And yes, the logo also made its way onto the spoon.

ATOMIC!

Atomicon is arguably the best sales and marketing conference in the world. It's an event like no other, with a buzzing community – a family of supportive, enthusiastic and creative entrepreneurs. It's the creation of Andrew (Pickering) and Pete (Gartland), with thousands flocking to the banks of the Tyne to experience the experience that is Atomicon.

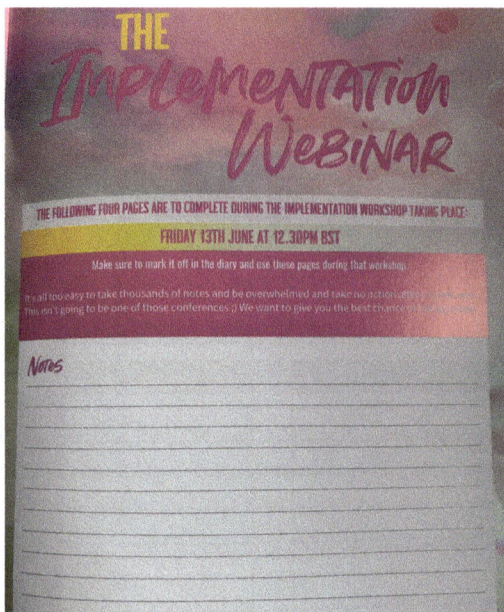

Now, I could talk about the stellar line-up of speakers, or the goody bags, or the stilt walkers, or the pre or after parties, or the sumptuous food, or the gorgeous Glasshouse venue, or maybe the continued online support before, during and after… I could go on.

Of course, Atomicon is a hive of digital expertise, but there is still a physical programme that awaits you in the goody bag. Towards the back of the programme, there are some Secret Sauce moments that make this event like no other. First, there's the 'Annoying Client Request' word search! And you can colour in Andrew and Pete, too. Then there's the 'People I've Met' section, plus you can also draw them too! But the big one is the implementation webinar, which all of the attendees can join after the event to make a plan of action from all of the hints, tips and advice received at the event.

This ensures commitment to momentum and longer-lasting value.

DRIVING HOME THE EXPERIENCE

One of the greatest and most memorable events I've been a part of was the wonderfully creative conference held by Green Motion, the environmentally friendly vehicle rental company. The venue they chose was right in the heart of Staffordshire – Alton Towers theme park, to be precise. Delegates from around the world came together with many of the teams bringing their families.

After the first day of the conference, everyone retreated to their hotel room to change for the evening dinner, which is where the Secret Sauce would be poured…

The park was closed (and the sun cream cart was fast asleep – you'll see this later in the book). The restaurant was a ten-minute walk away, but as we got closer we could hear that the rides were still in operation. There was no one there, but the rides were still open!

The team had organised exclusive use of the rides for the delegates and their families. It was like a Willy Wonka dream come true and something I bet we've all thought about at least once in our lives: 'I'd love to be the only one in this theme park.' Everyone loved it.

Oh, and we didn't just go to any restaurant. We were all booked into the rollercoaster-themed restaurant. This is where you order your food and, once it's ready, it travels on a rollercoaster car above your head, around the ceiling and then arrives at your table. Everyone loved it.

The Sauce continued to flow… I was speaking on day two, and after the conference, everyone retreated to their hotel room to change for the evening dinner. This time, we boarded coaches that took us to the other side of the theme park. We took part in a walking tour of the Towers, which featured street food and refreshments along the way. We arrived at the games section, with its basketball hoops and coconut shy. The games were all on free vend. We could throw as many times as we liked to win a prize (a very big prize). The area was full of smiling faces and ginormous cuddly toys sitting on the shoulders of the delegates. I had no idea how everyone was going to get back on the plane. Everyone loved it.

We arrived back at our hotel rooms and there on the dressing table was a Green Motion 'The Explorer' bear, with a passport inside featuring all of the countries this fantastic business is now operating in. I am going to guess that everyone loved this, too.

These ideas can set the tone of an event and become those Secret Sauce moments that teams, delegates and speakers will remember for a long, long time.

However, not everyone in the event space quite gets it. Not everyone spots opportunities to deliver Celebrity Service excellence and, unfortunately, these people jeopardise future bookings with event planners and professionals.

I am all for sharing positivity and inspiration, but there needs to be some balance at times and a sense of realism when it comes to service, or indeed the lack of it.

This will make your blood boil...

Q: HOW MUCH DOES A TEA BAG COST?

Two pence, five pence, ten pence? Or could you put a price of £50,000 on that little sachet of leaves?

As part of a client roadshow, I arrived the night before the big day and the events team had arrived as they always did, the day before, to set up the staging, rigging and layout of the room. Behind the scenes it was non-stop from dawn to dusk to get the room ready.

During set-up, the team told me they were desperate for a cuppa, so they asked the hotel for six cups of tea.

The hotel's response? 'You don't have any credit.'

'We'll pay,' came the reply.

'OK, we'll try to sort it out for you.'

Half an hour later, the teas arrived – with a bill for £55.

So how much does a tea bag cost?

For the love of boiling water, these conferences are crucial for the hospitality sector. Celebrity Service isn't just for guests – it's also for the events teams who have chosen your venue over your competitors.

WHAT WOULD YOU DO, GEOFF?

If I were the hotel events manager, I would pull out every stop to make my venue the most welcoming that any event company had experienced. I'd make it hotel policy that every event planner and AV team would have free tea and coffee during their stay, but most of all a big box of biscuits, which would already be wrapped up as a 'thank you' for choosing the venue – with a signed card as well.

The cost of a tea bag and some biscuits is minuscule when you consider the dozens of rooms that have been booked, the all-day room hire, as well as food and beverages for the entirety of the stay for hundreds of guests.

You want this team to come back again and again, and hopefully they'll bring their other clients with them, too.

This event team will never use that hotel venue again. Tens of thousands of pounds have slipped through the strainer.

There is not a general manager or team I've worked with who would dare deliver this level of service.

The name of the hotel will remain anonymous. I am here to lift up, not drag down. But I need to highlight the sheer lack of Celebrity Service and the oh-so-simple things you could do to attract next year's booking.

Chapter 7
A DASH OF RECOGNITION

RESPECT, CELEBRATE AND RECOGNISE

'It's increasingly difficult to recruit great people nowadays' and 'It's becoming harder to retain our greatest people' are two of the most popular comments I hear from business leaders and entrepreneurs.

With this in mind, I hope the following section will not only resonate but also help you.

A trio of words – respect, celebrate and recognise – will help increase your internal Celebrity Service experience for your team.

RESPECT

How do you show your current colleagues and teams that everyone matters in your organisation?

I saw one of the best signs you'll ever read while on a tour of the LKQ factory in Tamworth. This was the moment I realised this was a business that had its people at the heart of who they are and what they do.

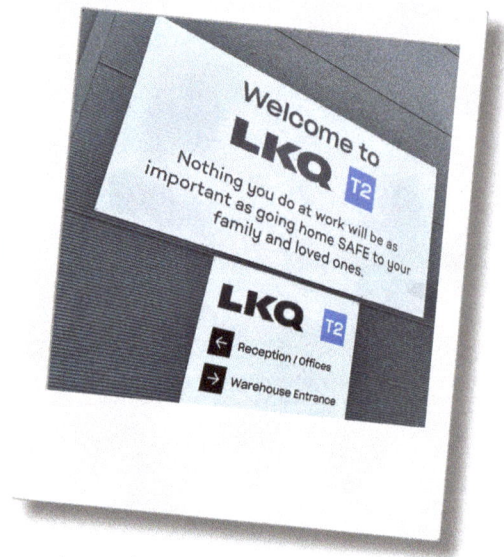

You are, of course, focused on the here and now with your current employees, as well as keeping an eye out for future talent. But what about those who are no longer with you? Should you forget about them entirely?

Outside the swimming pool area at Center Parcs in Whinfell Forest, Cumbria, I came across a row on park benches for guests to use – but one in particular stood out.

I love the fact that someone had this idea. I love the fact that Center Parcs loved the idea so much that they created this. And I love the fact that every guest and indeed every current employee at Center Parcs knows that they are respected, even when they are sadly no longer with us.

If I wanted to work somewhere where people were valued, this would draw me closer to a business.

Businesses and organisations that respect their teams often leave clues for you to see…

CELEBRATE

Timpson is a business that I have long admired. Whether you need passport photographs, a battery for your watch, a sole for your shoe or your three-piece suit dry cleaned, it's a business I love to visit – not just so that I can tell the time, or they can help me get through passport control, but because whenever I visit, I notice how they celebrate and how they look after, talk about and support their teams.

How do I know they celebrate the great things they do? They do not hide their Secret Sauce. Instead, they tell the world through posters that are hung above the counter, and in brochures for all the staff and customers to see, read and take away.

Even their strapline reads: 'Great Service by Great People'. Not too many companies will put the word 'people' into their branding.

How do you tell the world you really look after your people and provide an amazing place to work? I'd love to hear your ideas…

RECOGNISE

I have attended many awards dinners and gala evenings. As the desserts descend onto the tables, it's around this time that people are recognised for their contributions in the previous year.

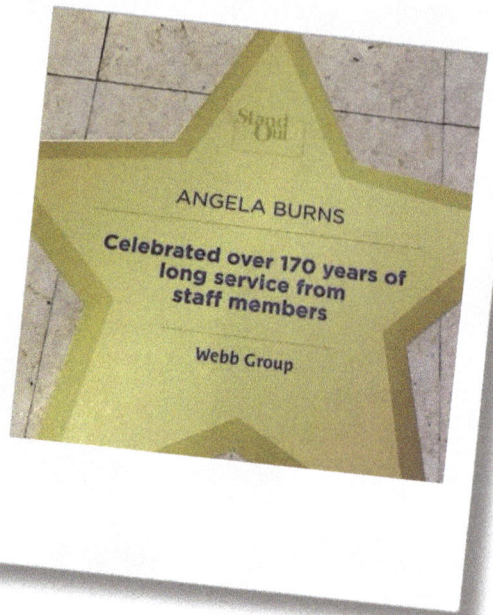

ANGELA BURNS

Celebrated over 170 years of long service from staff members

Webb Group

The shortlisted nominees will be read out before the winner is announced. The room erupts with applause, the person walks up, shakes hands, receives their award, smiles for the camera and returns to their seat before the next winner repeats the process.

Awards nights may differ, but the majority take this form. I love them, but in truth they are over in the blink of an eye.

One of my all-time favourites was at the Best Western conference in Brighton. It was a three-day event and they fully embraced the Celebrity Service theme.

To ensure they recognised their shortlisted nominees, they designed Hollywood Boulevard stars and stuck them onto the floors of the hotel where the conference was taking place. For three days, everyone could see the names of the nominees and read something about them.

To celebrate 85 years of Dublin Airport, a large, newspaper-style graphic was designed and displayed on the arrivals wall.

Everyone standing in arrivals to meet a loved one could read the graphic as they waited. The headline was the bit that spoke to me most, as it praises and recognises their amazing staff (first) and passengers (second).

How do you recognise the service superstars in your team?

Social media posts?

Awards and certificates?

Billboards?

Dedicated website pages?

Chapter 8
RED &
WRITE

CLEAN SHEET TO A LAST MINUTE WINNER

When your bank card expires, you cut it up into tiny pieces.

When your loyalty card no longer gives you rewards worth collecting, you cut it up into tiny pieces.

When the season card of your beloved favourite team comes to an end, you stay well away from the scissors!

That season card becomes a memento – a memory of torture and pain, of joy and ecstasy, of the season just gone. You keep the card as a souvenir, and it may even have its own special box alongside one-off cup final tickets, match day programmes and other memorabilia.

This is a story of two halves...

Our Sunderland AFC season cards arrive in the post. As per usual, they have all our details on the reverse – name, customer number, category, stand, turnstile, row, seat and block. On the front is a splash of red and white with the club crest. Just your normal season card that will make its way into a memory box in May. Everything is good.

The following season, our cards arrive in the post, but this time, there is something missing. Our details are all there as before, but on the reverse there is no splash of colour, no club crest. It is technically blank. Inside the envelope is a printed note that says...

SIGNED, SEALED, DELIVERED

Here it is, your Sunderland AFC season card.

We can only apologise that your card is not branded. Unfortunately, this is due to printing issues with our provider. To make this up to you, your card has been signed by one of the first-team squad.

We look forward to sharing the remainder of the season with you and thank you for your support.

Ha'way the Lads!

We later discovered that there was an issue with the printers. But instead of sending out the card as it was, the club had asked some of its players to personally sign the season card for the fans. We now had the autograph of our left back, No 17, Dennis Cirkin. How fantastic was that? In all honesty, it was so much better than the printed version. Now we had a real keepsake – a signed, personalised card from one of our idols – and yes, you've guessed it, something to shout about in this book.

Within your business, life is always going to throw you a curveball, but it's how you take that negative and spin it into a better experience that gives you your Secret Sauce.

Chapter 9
POPCORN 'N' CHILL

LIGHTS, CAMERA, EXPERIENCE!

You may not believe this, but James Bond actor Daniel Craig and I share something in common. We both had to wait until our big performance could be seen on the big screen.

Unusually, the producers of the 2021 movie *No Time to Die* decided against early home release and delayed the launch until everyone could enjoy it safely in the best place possible – the cinema.

I was just about to go to contract to speak at the national Cineworld conference when the Covid-19 curtain came down. A real shame, as my family are big fans of the movies and especially our local Cineworld in Boldon – and I had tons of tailor-made content.

Then, in 2022, at the O2 in London, the curtain rose and everyone was back, including Mr Craig and Mr Ramm…

Around 95 per cent of the time, I start my keynote talks in the same way. I ask a big opening question and love to have everyone engaged and participating from the off.

Not that day, though. At the conference, I changed the entire start. I walked on and announced to everyone, 'We are going to have a very special quiz – with prizes, of course.' It was going to be just as engaging, with everyone joining in.

Question number one: 'Name the very first movie you ever went to see at the cinema.'

Dozens of hands went up, with some fantastic answers. I shared with the audience that my first movie was *Flash Gordon*.

Question number two: 'Name the very first movie you went to see on your first date with your partner/husband/wife.'

Dozens of hands went up, with some hilarious answers, including someone shouting out *Fifty Shades of Grey* – and they were still together. I revealed that mine and Hayley's was *Broken Arrow*.

Question number three: 'Name the very first movie you watched on Netflix.'

Not one hand went up. I didn't know either.

Question number four: 'Name the very first movie you watched with your partner/husband/wife on Amazon Prime or Disney+.'

Again, not one hand went up.

I paused and then delivered the most important line of my keynote.

'Netflix, Disney+, Rakuten and Prime are all brilliant, and they all sell movies. But ONLY you, ONLY your cinema and ONLY your team can create an experience your customers will remember for the rest of their lives.'

I then proceeded to share the 'Play it again, Sam' story…

PLAY IT AGAIN, SAM

Remember taking those first steps in the post-Covid world? The ones where you could get back to doing 'normal' things like eating in a restaurant, sitting on a train or going to the cinema?

When everyone slowly returned, they did so with hesitancy but also with a tinge of excitement and an urge to claw back some of the experiences they'd missed out on.

For Elliot's birthday, we didn't want to just to surprise him with a normal trip to the cinema, but instead, having missed out on so much popcorn, the boat was pushed out further than normal. So we took him for a VIP experience at Cineworld York.

You have your own VIP lounge with huge, reclining leather seats and free hot dogs, drinks, coffees, sweets and popcorn (according to Elliot!).

From the moment we entered the foyer, the Cineworld team were superb – happy, welcoming and polite. I'd also extend this to the help and support we had received via Facebook Messenger prior to booking (not every organisation is so readily available on social media).

It was lovely to see that there were no signs of 'rustiness' or excuses after long-term furlough here.

We arrived at the VIP room. Wow.

A young gentleman called Sam walked up to us. He introduced himself during elbow bumps and then asked for our names (we'd never experienced this in any cinema). He then used them at various points of our visit. He asked if this was a special occasion, so Elliot said it was his birthday.

Sam's focus was solely on Elliot. He must have called him by his name at least three times – so simple, yet so rare.

He made this special visit special.

The seats, huge screens and food will always add to an experience, but finding out a name and then using it when the time is right is what makes it a true Celebrity Service experience with added Secret Sauce.

VUE TO A THRILL

How you respond to customers can improve or diminish their experience. Ignore them at your peril. Respond using artificial intelligence if you must, but responding with thought and creativity will always be remembered.

I was due to deliver a talk for the general managers of Vue at their brand new cinema in Nottingham. So, to conduct a little research, we went to see the tyre-burning blockbuster *F1*.

We ordered a milkshake, coffees and popcorn from two amazing members of staff. The person serving our milkshake said, 'And here are two straws, as the first one will become soggy.' This was a brilliant line. They know the issues people have with paper straws, so she offered a solution before the problem became a problem.

The movie finished and it was brilliant. So much so, that I took to social media to recommend seeing it on the big screen. And then I tagged Vue, wondering if they would respond.

This is brilliant.

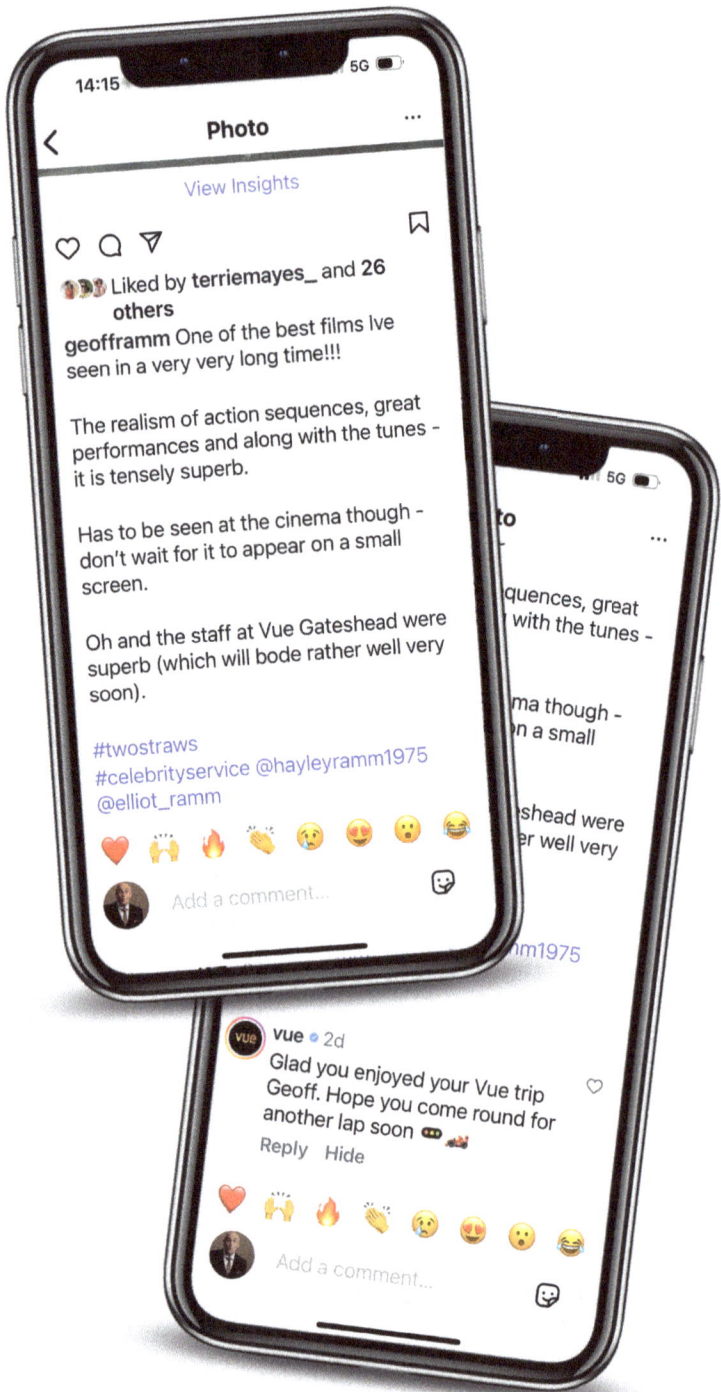

Liked by **terriemayes_** and **26** others

geofframm One of the best films Ive seen in a very very long time!!!

The realism of action sequences, great performances and along with the tunes - it is tensely superb.

Has to be seen at the cinema though - don't wait for it to appear on a small screen.

Oh and the staff at Vue Gateshead were superb (which will bode rather well very soon).

#twostraws #celebrityservice @hayleyramm1975 @elliot_ramm

Add a comment...

vue • 2d

Glad you enjoyed your Vue trip Geoff. Hope you come round for another lap soon 🎬🏎️

Reply   Hide

Add a comment...

EXPERIENCE MAKERS:
MOVIE MAGIC

Is there anything better than sitting down with a bucket of warm popcorn, ready to watch the latest blockbuster on the big screen? The lights go down, the trailers begin, and you're transported into another world.

As you now know, we had a brilliant experience on Elliot's birthday and the staff were fantastic, but if you and your team had been there, could you have gone a step further?

Let's see with this next Experience Makers challenge.

You and your team own a cinema. A family book their tickets and tell you in advance that it's one of their children's birthdays.

This challenge is in two parts.

*   How can you deliver a great customer experience for them on arrival?
*   What can you do for them just as they are about to leave?

Lights, camera – now let's action some Celebrity Service blockbuster moments to have them talking about you for years to come.

Good luck.

WHAT WOULD YOU DO, GEOFF?

When it's a special occasion, most people are desperate to capture the moment. That's why couples spend a fortune on photographers. It's why fans of artists and bands will watch the show through their smartphones rather than be in the moment. And it's the reason why theme parks will take a picture of your blurred, screaming face and sell it back to you minutes after the ride has finished. We simply want to capture and then remember this one-off occasion.

If I were to run my own cinema, I'd set up a dedicated area to take photographs in the foyer. Maybe I'd set up a scene with a director's chair and an old-style megaphone and clapperboard (you can write the person's name or age on here too). I'd take a photograph of the family as they arrived and, while they were watching the movie, I'd print the photograph and slot it in a frame or sleeve with my cinema branding in the corner. A member of the team would then wait for them to come out to give them their FREE gift. Oh, sorry – I forgot to mention it would be free.

I know this isn't business protocol – you know, charge them, then charge them again – but this would only cost pennies and would stay on their fridge or shelf at home for the next few years. I think I could offset this experience as marketing!

I'd also have a large, branded card that the team and I could sign. The inside would remain blank as we could personalise it to any situation or theme or words to the film the family were watching.

The Secret Sauce would not only be making it personal, but also the free gift at the end, which, let's be honest, no other cinema chain would have thought of.

COULD WE HAVE SOME SPRINKLES ON OUR SECRET SAUCE, PLEASE?

The devil is in the detail, such as what appears to be normal linen on your bed at the Hard Rock Hotel, until you zoom in to take a closer look…

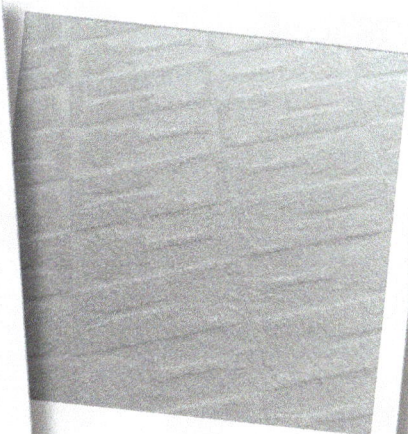

The Lakeside Inn pub at Center Parcs has a goody bag of treats for every four-legged friend.

Beside the children's play area at Alton Towers theme park, there is a cart full of factor 30 sun cream (in case you have forgotten yours or have run out). Oh, and it's free!

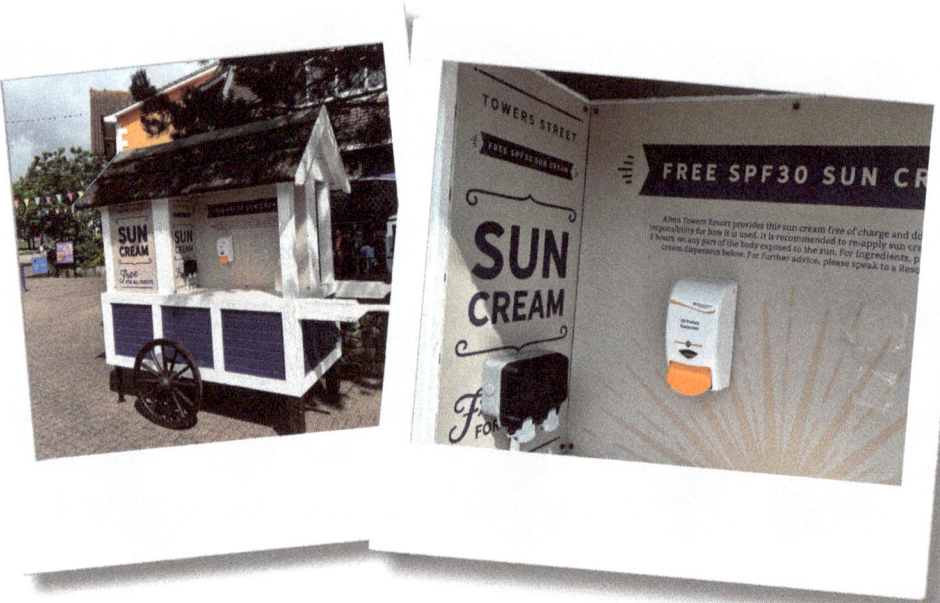

At the amazing Allegiant Stadium, home to the Las Vegas Raiders, they have installed drinks holders and phone chargers so that fans can watch the game, recharge their phones and put their drinks down without spillages. Oh, and as with so many attractions, you exit via the store. However, the lanyard around your neck gives you 10 per cent off all merchandise!

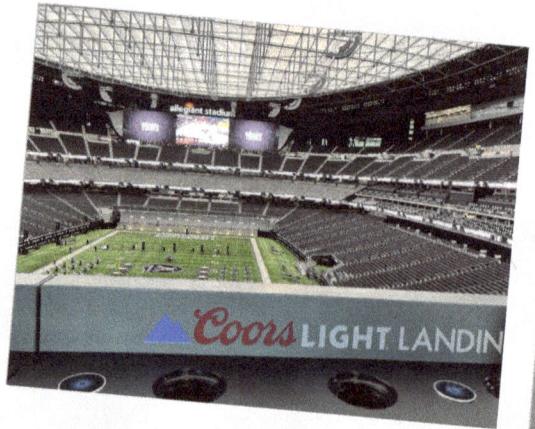

And if you thought having your name on your coffee cup was good, check these out…

These works of art are all down to Ewa, a barista for Starbucks at Village Hotels in Elstree, Hertfordshire.

Good service is writing your name correctly on a cup. Celebrity Service is always a level up…

Cooking the books…
To welcome me to the
Citystars hotel in
Cairo, the team left a
copy of my book on
the table in my room.
But this was no
ordinary book – the
kitchen team made it
into a cake!

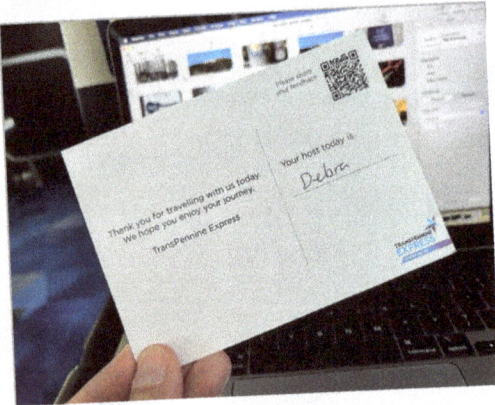

To thank passengers for
choosing to travel with
TransPennine Express,
they receive a card
during the journey.

THE PASSION OF ATLÉTICO MADRID

At the Riyadh Air Metropolitano Stadium, home to Spanish LaLiga side Atlético Madrid, the words CORAJE and CORAZÓN (meaning 'courage' and 'heart') are displayed on the walls of the tunnel. These words define the club's identity and are part of their anthem.

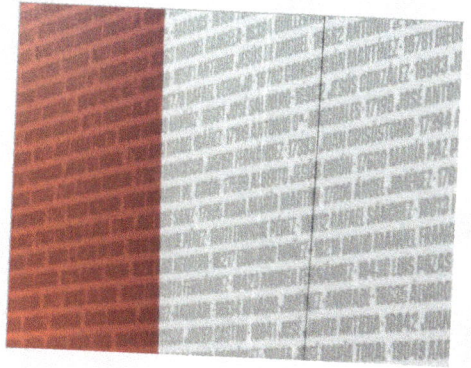

From a distance, this looks impressive, but when you walk over to take a closer look, it becomes mightily impressive.

There are more than 126,000 members of the club, and every name, surname and membership number has been included on the walls.

As this will be the last thing the players see before every home game, they'll feel the support of the thousands of members the club has around the world.

After the stadium and museum tour ends, and as with any other attraction, you have to exit through the store. And while browsing the merchandise, if you want to try anything on, then let me recommend going to the changing rooms…

EXPERIENCE MAKERS:
'HO HO OH'

Let's leave behind the ideas of the PAST – it's time to create an incredible PRESENT that will become an amazing FUTURE experience for your colleagues, customers and suppliers.

The gift of Christmas is an opportunity to say a very big thank you and to appreciate the support you have received this year whether you are a colleague or a customer.

How do you say Merry Christmas? And more importantly…

For your colleagues – how do you say 'thank you' for their hard work and endeavour this year?

For your customers – how do you say 'thank you' for the business this year?

For your suppliers and fans – how do you say 'thank you' for their recommendations and referrals?

And here's the extra, tricky, bonus challenge – what can you do on zero budget?

Not everyone can be seen to spend money, but I'm sure your team can come up with one or two wonderful ideas when they come together to become Experience Makers.

Good luck.

Chapter 10
STARS OF THE STARS AND STRIPES

SMALL MOMENTS, BIG MEMORIES

CHICAGO CARES

It can take a while to come across a great Celebrity Service moment, but in one single day in my now favourite city, Chicago, I came across two!!!

First, say hello to Maria. She works at Marriott Bonvoy, part of the Marriott group of hotels. While all the staff were excellent, Maria exuded extra energy, enthusiasm and an eye for a great service experience, which these days is a rare treat – meeting, greeting and helping every guest at the rather sumptuous breakfast lounge.

Day one. As I queued for my scrambled eggs, Maria walked past and said, 'Oh, love the shirt.' Of course she did – it was my lucky Sunderland Wembley play-off final top! I said, 'Thank you,' and she picked up on my non-American accent. We chatted about where I was from and what I was doing there, and she said she had lived in London with her family a while back.

The next morning, Maria recognised me and said, 'Good morning, Geoff.' Ten minutes later, she came over and asked about my plans for the day. Having completed the Soldier Field and Hard Rock visits the day before, I was planning to go back into the city centre to have a mooch around the riverside and to also check out the Cook County Building (which features at the end of the infamous chase scene in the Blues Brothers movie, when the Bluesmobile eventually implodes before Jake and Ellwood run into the building to meet Steven Spielberg).

She said, 'Follow me,' and we walked over to the window. 'Right there is the bus stop, and you can take the No 3 into town.'

You wait for one Celebrity Service moment to come along and then two arrive at once.

The No 3 bus pulled up. I put one foot on the step and, with a huge, beaming smile, the driver said: 'Welcome on board, sir. How are you?'

THIS HAS NOT HAPPENED ON ANY OTHER BUS I HAVE TAKEN.

'I am very well – how are you?'

I tapped on the cardless machine, and it didn't work. I tried again. The same. A lady shouted down the bus: 'You need a special card.' I didn't have a special card. I did have a $10 note, but there was no change available, as it's all automated.

The driver: 'Please, sir, please don't worry. Have a seat and hey, you can buy a card tomorrow or maybe the next day. But for now, let me take you to where you want to go.'

I walked down the busy bus and alighted at the back when my stop arrived, to follow in the footsteps of Jake and Ellwood. My only regret is that I did not get the bus driver's name. But I did take a photo as the bus was pulling away, and if you look very closely you can see his beaming smile before he gave me the thumbs-up.

If you know this driver, please thank him on my behalf and tell him he's now in a book!

Here's the Secret Sauce. Take an interest. Compliment. Remember. Help people to get to where they want to go. And don't worry about the money, just give someone a lift today that they will be eternally grateful for.

SPRINKLING THE STARDUST...

If you were to search online for the top places to go in New York, you would see the usual names appearing, from the Statue of Liberty, Empire State Building, One World Observatory and Rockefeller Center to the Brooklyn Bridge, Wall Street, Times Square and Central Park. All of them are world-famous, iconic structures and destinations. However, there is also another 'top place' that is regularly mentioned, and it's not your usual tourist attraction. In fact, it's a restaurant at 1650 Broadway.

Yes, you read that right – the restaurant is the attraction.

Imagine for one moment that you owned this restaurant. And for seven days a week, from the sun rising at 7 am until you closed the doors at midnight, you had customers patiently queuing around the block to come in.

What do you think you would have to offer to create such a phenomenal demand? A celebrity chef, perhaps? The world's greatest food? The world's cheapest or most expensive food? Or how about stunning panoramic views as you dine?

There are approximately 26,000 restaurants in New York, so what would be your Secret Sauce to help you stand out from the competition and attract and maintain this level of customer demand? It seems that all you need do is provide something nobody else is doing: entertainment.

Let me introduce you to Ellen's Stardust Diner – a restaurant so popular that when I mentioned it on my socials, my post lit up, with many of my connections having also been there and loved the experience.

I only knew of the place when my daughter pointed out that on every video she watched about the best places to eat in New York, Ellen's was always in the top ten places to visit! I stress that it was in every video she watched!

So if everyone says, 'You must go here,' then we do.

Arriving at 8.42 am, we queued for 20 minutes. When we set foot in the restaurant we looked around and saw that every cover was taken. We walked upstairs and took our seats at the one remaining table. And then it started, with one of the waitresses belting out 'This Will Be' by Natalie Cole.

Not a minute had passed before a waiter and waitress duet jumped up onto the tables and sang the John Travolta and Olivia Newton-John classic 'You're the One That I Want'. This was quickly followed by their rendition of 'Summer Nights'.

We were transfixed – as was every other diner, as the singers/ waiters walked around each table, used the catwalk area downstairs before ascending upstairs, and basically used every square inch of the restaurant to put on a show for everyone. (Please note, this was still breakfast time.)

Observing the other diners, I noticed that three things were happening:

- Every diner was joining in with the song.
- As they ate, every diner held in their hands both a fork and their phone, while recording the experience (and I wonder what they would do with those images and videos?).
- Every diner had a huge smile on their face.

This was special, and it continued…

I noticed that one of the waitresses at the till was ringing in the checks, taking cash from customers and handing out their change, all while clamping the microphone into her neck during 'Walking on Sunshine' by Katrina and the Waves and then 'Late Night Talking' by Harry Styles. Even when you are flat-out busy, you can always find a way to deliver an experience.

You would think the Secret Sauce at Ellen's would be the entertainment, and you would be right, but I believe there is an even better recipe for their success. What surprised us was the number of songs the team were performing. This wasn't a performance every 20 or 30 minutes – this was one song after another after another.

In between our pancakes, breakfast burrito and eggs Benedict, we also had…

'Watermelon Sugar' (by Harry 'they love you in the US' Styles).

'Can't Take My Eyes Off You' (by Andy Williams).

And to round off our breakfast, 'Circle of Life' (from *The Lion King*). The best part of this performance was that another four team members supported the lead singer by holding up brooms with animals heads on top!

We left full, we left smiling, we left with an experience, we left and told a lot of people about it.

It's also wonderfully old school, as you can't ring to book, you can't go online to secure a table, you just have to turn up, wait in line and get ready to be entertained.

I'm amazed that there isn't an Ellen's in London's West End. Maybe that's an idea for someone reading this?

The entertainment, the consistency and the ability to support your colleagues in providing an experience like no other will get you talked about and featured in other people's posts, reviews and of, course, books! That's Ellen's Secret Sauce.

If you'd like to watch a montage of some of the greatest hits I recorded, just scan the QR code.

Enjoy.

WE'RE LOVING IT…

Every once in a while, someone comes along and changes the game.

The truth is that I'd never thought about writing a third Celebrity Service book until I came across Zack.

Grace and Elliot said they'd never been to a McDonald's in America before and wanted to experience the difference. So we left one of the Disney theme parks, ordered a taxi and headed to the nearest restaurant.

At the time of writing, there are tens of thousands of McDonald's restaurants in the world with more than 100,000 company employees (not including franchises). And the person you are about to meet is, for me, the greatest employee of them all.

We entered the Golden Arches at 1596 West Buena Vista Drive, Kissimmee, and delivered our best impression of Tom Cruise in Minority Report, as we waved our hands across the interactive ordering screen. We made our choices and were asked if we'd like to collect at the counter or have the food delivered to a table.

With weary Disney feet, we sat down at a table and awaited the delivery of our food and drink.

Moments later, we heard a sound. Both Grace and I looked up, glanced at each other and smiled. A few seconds later, we heard the sound again. This time we all looked up and could make out that it was coming from the counter. We weren't quite sure what we were hearing, but the customers collecting their food had a big smile on their faces as they were walking away. The next time it happened, we tuned in and started to laugh. It was coming from one person behind the counter who was passing over orders to the customers.

What was going on?

Having consumed our food and drink, Grace and Elliot fancied a McFlurry ice cream.

'Shall we order to our table or at the counter?'

'At the counter,' I said, wanting to get closer to find out what was really going on.

We were third in line and now had a prime-time view.

Every time a customer came to the counter to collect their order, Zack would walk over with their food and, as he was passing it to them, delivered an impression. It just so happened that today was Mickey Mouse day.

He'd talk to the customer in this voice, and they loved it, we loved it, and by the look on Zack's face, he loved it too. It was hilarious.

Grace and I were next up, so I asked him, 'Do you do this for every customer?'

'Yes,' he said.

He told me he had done this for 20 years. It all started when he was gaming online. He'd deliver his impressions through his headset. Then he brought his impressions into work, and now impersonates more than 30 characters.

Incredibly, he also told me he had given up numerous promotions within McDonald's. I asked why, and his answer was perfect: 'Because I'd have to give up doing this for every customer.'

You would think Zack's Secret Sauce was the unique impressions – and you'd be right. However, there is also the key area of consistency to consider here. He didn't pick and choose which customer he did it for – it was for everyone! Plus, I have to congratulate the management for allowing Zack to do this. There is so much red tape around what staff can and can't say, so to allow this form of independence was fantastic to see.

Oh, you didn't think I would just share this story without you being able to hear Zack's amazing impression, did you? Before the ice creams arrived, I asked Zack if I could record him passing over the order to Grace. If you'd like to watch it, just scan this QR code.

Enjoy.

Chapter 11

YOUR FIVE WORD STRATEGY

KEEP THE SERVICE SPARK ALIVE

To help and support you and your team in creating and maintaining a Celebrity Service experience, I use this very simple yet powerful five-word strategy to help you build the momentum for long-term success.

The five words are: time, space, ideas, action and recognition.

TIME

A question I'm often asked is, 'What is the biggest mistake businesses make when it comes to customer service?' Although my brain and tongue want to go into overdrive at this point, I have to default to the biggest mistake of all: time. Or, dare I say, the lack of it.

Let me explain.

QUESTION: When was your last leadership meeting? (It might have been last month.)

QUESTION: When is your next sales meeting? (It could well be every Tuesday.)

QUESTION: When is your next customer service meeting? (Insert tumbleweed here.)

We all know the importance of service and delivering a great experience for our clients and customers (it's why you are reading this book), but do we give it the time it deserves?

The area of 'customer service' can often be shoehorned into the 'any other business' section of an agenda. I should know, I've seen it many times.

You need to dedicate time. With this time, you can gather your team to discuss, dissect and inspire one another with service ideas, issues and opportunities. The length is similar in age to the question, 'How long is a piece of string?' – but for starters, have one 15-minute meeting a week or a fortnight – maybe an hour a month. Whatever time frame and frequency you choose, you must stick with bringing everyone together on a specific date and time (in person or virtually). But one swallow doesn't make a summer. You must be consistent with this (even when you think there is nothing to add this week).

SPACE

One of my favourite ideas is to create a visual reminder of what Celebrity Service looks like.

Gather evidence on your smartphone, take photographs and record videos of someone or something that has stopped you in your tracks in terms of the service and experience you have just had.

Now take this evidence and print it, share it and post it in a place where everyone can see it.

I call this the 'Celebrity Service Wall', a space solely for inspiration. You have dedicated much-needed time; now it's about dedicating a space to remind you and your team of what incredible looks like.

This area will be full of little Secret Sauce moments from all industries and sectors.

And once you start to fill the space, encourage everyone to add to the wall. And when you have your next meeting, sit next to this area to discuss these ideas and see how they could help serve you and your own customers.

IDEAS

I know that by reading and participating in the 120 Challenges and Experience Makers tasks, you will be fully armed and loaded with the tools and techniques to generate wonderfully creative, sometimes obvious and simply amazing ideas to deliver a better service.

Within the time and space you have dedicated, you now have those crucial ideas to roll out.

However, some of these ideas may be illegal (maybe don't choose those), some may require a lot of financial investment (maybe introduce those later), but some of those ideas will be gems. And it's this handful of gems/ideas that you can pick and then develop further before you introduce them into your business.

ACTION

Take your handful of gems.

Pick one.

Just one.

If you introduce too many at once, it will be like spinning too many plates at the same time. Some will spin, others may wobble and some may fall. And there is nothing worse than coming up with a good idea and seeing it smash to the ground.

So introduce your chosen idea into your business and let it grow until it becomes a part of your service culture. Once it's bedded in, introduce your second idea and repeat the process. Over time, this creates the gap in your service you never knew existed.

One idea at a time won't overtax your team, it will be manageable and therefore easier to deliver, monitor and analyse.

RECOGNITION

Who came up with the idea? Who developed the idea further? Who introduced it? Who is now delivering on this idea?

Quite simply, recognise the people in your team who are shaping the Celebrity Service experience with the ideas they have created.

Don't wait until the end of the year at awards night or until your next board meeting. Do it now. Recognise the individual, recognise the team.

BONUS

As a bonus to the five-word strategy, I would recommend purchasing a 'calendar of opportunities' (which could be placed in your space). Your wall planner for the coming year can be filled with many opportunities and important dates.

These could include colleagues' birthdays, important client dates, start dates of your ideas, and even the annual customer service week. Admit it, that's never written down and only thought about when you see a post explaining customer service week started… yesterday!

Your calendar of opportunities keeps you on track and focused for the year ahead.

Fill it. Use it.

NB: I shared this one technique with the wonderful entrepreneurs and consultants at Avon – their successes were simply off the chart they were filling in!

Chapter 12

WHAT HAPPENED NEXT?

THE CELEBRITY SERVICE EFFECT

From the moment I launched my business, I have always said the best part of delivering Celebrity Service keynotes and interactive sessions are the results that the entrepreneurs, high-performance teams and organisations go on to achieve.

Whether it's a 20-minute TED-style blitz from the main stage or a deeper, day-long event where we create game-changing ideas, essentially it's all about results.

When audiences hear the inspirational stories and action the award-winning techniques, they achieve long-term success.

Results and successes are varied, from higher NPS (net promoter scores) to Tripadvisor reviews, from sector awards and honours to greater employee engagement, and from contracts won to increased revenues.

When you, your team, brand or organisation embrace Celebrity Service, you win.

A fun fact about my business is that I never receive enquiries from companies or organisations that are struggling with their service experience. I only ever receive calls and enquiries from those that are already pretty good (7 or 8 out of 10) but want to go further in their pursuit of becoming number one in their sector.

This next section is dedicated to a rather wonderful selection of businesses that I've worked with and, after the keynote or interactive session, have gone on to discover the gap they never knew existed.

STRIP OFF

If my memory (and Google search history) serves, then the very first Sunderland football match I ever attended was on 3 April 1985. I stood in the Roker End under the floodlights with my best mate and his dad. Despite a 3-0 defeat, I was hooked.

To say that the journey has been a rollercoaster would be the understatement of understatements. I've witnessed the highest of highs and the lowest of lows. But it's a love. It's a passion. It's my passion.

During my college and university days, I worked at the Roker Park Suite serving the directors, players and sponsors. It was my dream job during my further educational days.

Now I'm running my speaking business, if I were to think of a perfect client to work alongside, Porsche and the Las Vegas Raiders would be pretty unreal. But my ultimate client would, of course, be Sunderland AFC.

And then it happened – a rather surreal half-day Celebrity Service keynote and interactive session live at the Stadium of Light. It was an experience I will never forget, and the biggest business bucket list item ticked off.

While I could wax lyrical about my history with the club (which I guess I may have just done), this next story is dedicated to the marketing team who, within hours, took on board a 120 Challenge and created a poster to deliver a great experience.

Let me wax lyrical one more time. Back in 1992, our away strip was a gorgeous white with green and navy blue trim. In that same season, we also got to the FA Cup final and, as was tradition at that time, both finalists would release a cup final single. The song Sunderland chose to cover was 'Ain't No Stopping Us Now' by McFadden and Whitehead (not to be confused with James or Dean).

Fast forward more than three decades, and the iconic strip design was brought back. This was going to be huge. And indeed it was, as fans queued around the club store and the strips outsold the kit of Champions League winners, Paris Saint-Germain!

To prepare for the launch, the team had got together and had their very own 120 Challenge, with their focus on the words they could use to print on the 'coming soon' style poster. Rather than just putting up a sign that said, 'We are now closed for the launch' or, 'Kit launch tomorrow', they did this…

The club's Ben Roberts sent me the photograph and our conversation on Messenger went like this:

Ben: '120 Challenge – the marketing team took on board your wisdom.'

Me: 'Hey, Ben – that is just brilliant!!!'

Ben: 'The team couldn't have done it without you.'

Me: 'We are going to create some real magic this coming year. Please congratulate the team from me.'

Ben: 'I will, mate.'

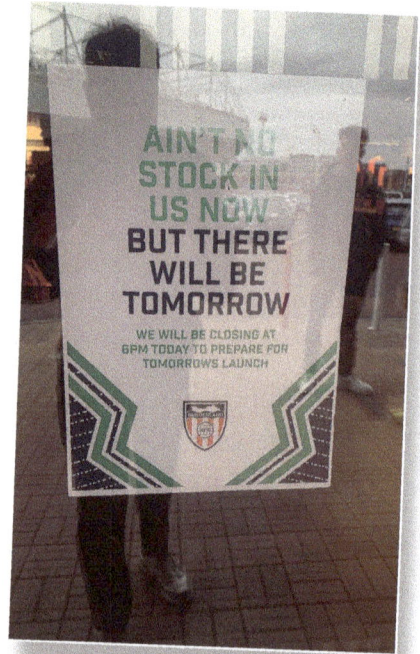

The words you choose to use can help you deliver your Secret Sauce, and yet again the 120 technique delivered a great experience for the fans.

SLINGSHOT TO SUCCESS

I'd delivered a global virtual event for voco hotels alongside Julie Cheesman (you may remember her interview in Celebrity Service Superstars), but wasn't quite sure how the message would land via a screen from the north-east of England to Asia. However, I was about to find out, as a year later I was at voco Orchard in Singapore to deliver a live event.

Before the staff training day started, the area general manager Mark Winterton and hotel manager Walid Ouezini took me on a tour of the hotel. In particular, they wanted to show me the basement. It was not what I was expecting.

After our 75-minute virtual event the year before, they had gone on to create their very own Celebrity Service corridor – wall after wall after wall of inspiring ideas, wonderful guest feedback, upcoming birthdays and, most importantly, team recognition for their ideas and delivery. You name it, every poster along this very long corridor was focused on the hotel delivering a Celebrity Service experience to each other and every guest. Oh, and strangely, there was even a photograph of me on the desk where they hold their service meetings (I am always looking – ha ha!).

But then came the results of our day and, a couple of months later, I received the following email from Mark…

Hi Geoff

Hope you are well and Happy belated wedding anniversary!

Thought I would let you see how Cosmo is getting on… He's exhausted and is having a week of 'Me Time'

He's been extremely busy with us since he joined the team back in August and has been working with each department every month where he's supported new initiatives, raised awareness, shared best practices and even met guests!

Our Guest Love score is now 84 YTD which is a whopping 14 points up on the end of the first year and we are Green for the first time ever.

M

Mark Winterton
Area General Manager Singapore
General Manager voco Orchard Singapore

STRATHALLAN SCHOOL

Having received the brilliantly personalised covering letter and prospectus in the weeks leading up to the event at Strathallan, I was not surprised at what the team went on to create after our Celebrity Inset Service day in Perthshire, Scotland…

Your visit has made my job easier in terms of getting the message out that, while we are a school, we are also a business that has customers.

Below are some changes…

We have a Polaroid camera and printer to capture moments from prospective pupils' taster days to send home with them. We also use it for special moments with current pupils, for example, international pupils wearing a kilt. We also send these to their parents and agents digitally.

We are looking at changing the experience for those requesting a prospectus from outside the UK, who currently don't receive the printed version. We're looking at what we can do to create the 'magic moment' for them, and we are planning to implement personalised videos (beyond what we currently do) as part of our shift to the new website.

We have instigated personal calls to parents from a member of the senior management team one week after their child has started – to check that they have what they need and iron out any niggles early on.

After the new year had started and the girls were settled, I took some pictures of my new tutor group. I had two of the photos (standing outside Glenbrae* and one of them jumping) made into a postcard. These were sent with a 'welcome to third form Glenbrae' to the parents of all of my tutees. I wanted them to have a personalised and physical reminder of the start of senior school for their child and as part of Glenbrae.

Glenbrae had welcome cards made for each new start with a handwritten message from the head of house as well as congrats cards for commendations and distinctions. New pupils also receive a purple bag of goodies to start them off (purple is the house colour), pen, highlighter, sweeties, etc, in a purple bag.

What we have been able to do is quote Celebrity Service, which takes the heat out of a discussion where someone has perhaps missed the mark, to make it less personal!

Claire Bath, director of external relations

(*One of Strathallan's girls' boarding houses.)

LKQ

And you thought Amazon were fast to deliver? Meet LKQ and the millions of auto parts ready to be dispatched to your nearest garage, ready to have you back on the road.

I've been fortunate enough to work alongside this fantastic team in the UK, Europe and North America. Here are a few examples of what they did right after the events.

LKQ Euro Car Parts Barnstaple Branch

The team at Barnstaple Branch have been gifting Easter hamper baskets to valued customers - a thoughtful way to show appreciation and deliver a personal thank you for their loyalty. Now that's Celebrity Service!

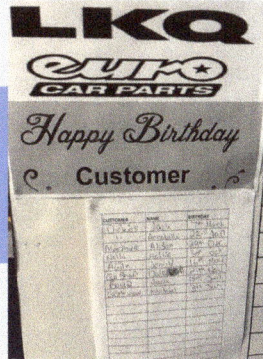

Wakefield celebrates customer birthdays

The Wakefield Team have started a growing list of customer birthdays, sending each one a card on their special day. One customer was so touched by the gesture that they called the branch from a sun lounger in Spain to say thank you!

Keep up the 'Celebrity Service' Wakefield.

LKQ UK and Ireland   10   Keeping you moving

Dundalk Branch Celebrating with our Customers

A customer of the Dundalk branch got married in March and Ben Appley, AM, and Pauline Markey, Admin, made a hamper to congratulate the happy couple!

Great to see the relationship between branch and customer going from strength to strength.

LKQ UK and Ireland   7   Keeping you moving

AVON CALLED, AVON CREATED, AVON CELEBRATED… SUCCESS

Having already spoken at the Avon leaders' conference, I was rebooked to deliver at the main conference just a few months later. I would go on to deliver three virtual sessions over three months to build on the momentum.

A private Facebook group was launched and hundreds of amazing ideas were shared of what people had created and actioned, as well as the results they achieved. To help you track and share your great ideas, I urge you to do the same with your business and your teams.

Back to what happened next…

At the main conference, I delivered a keynote in the morning, and my good friend Sara Davies MBE spoke in the afternoon. Seven hundred people were there that day, including Hall of Fame representative and bronze executive leader, Dawn Fazackerly. Dawn was speaking before me on the main stage, sharing her inspirational journey with Avon.

I had no idea that a portion of her brilliant and emotional talk would include me. In the months since seeing me at our first event, Dawn revealed that her profits had doubled after the changes she made to her service!!! I repeat, doubled.

This is her story…

A reflection on the partners' event in Solihull, September 2024

Celebrity Service is not about extravagance or grand gestures – it is about small, meaningful acts that make a customer feel valued. Geoff's vision reminded me that creating memorable encounters is a powerful way to build lasting relationships and trust.

I couldn't help but feel inspired to bring the concept of Celebrity Service to my own customers. While the idea seemed ambitious at first, Geoff's practical advice made it approachable and achievable.

I began brainstorming ideas about how I could implement this philosophy in my own business. Could I personalise my communication more effectively? Could I surprise my customers with thoughtful gestures that they wouldn't expect? Geoff's teachings left my mind buzzing with possibilities. I realised that offering Celebrity Service is not about reinventing the wheel – it's about shifting perspectives and recognising the opportunities for greatness in everyday moments.

As I drove home after the event, my mind was racing. The concept of Celebrity Service had sparked a fire within me, urging me to explore new ways to connect with my customers. What could I do to make them feel valued, appreciated and truly special? How could I emulate the principles Geoff had shared and create a culture of excellence in my own business?

The key to success lies in authenticity and consistency. Celebrity Service is not a one-time effort – it's a mindset that must be woven into the fabric of an organisation.

By treating everyone equally and finding creative ways to enhance their experience, businesses can foster loyalty, trust and admiration.

It's not just about offering a service – it's about creating an experience, a memory and a moment that customers will cherish.

Impact on my business

Overview of business growth

The impact on my business over the past year has been remarkable, marked by significant milestones, strategic achievements and consistent growth. By leveraging innovative approaches and maintaining a strong focus on customer engagement, I have managed to create a thriving and evolving business.

Direct Seller of the Year 2025 (Direct Selling Association).

Here are a few of the simple changes I made:

- *Packaging – created with attention to detail = customers really want to open it.*

- *Planning key dates = Valentine's, Mother's Day, Father's Day, as examples.*

- *My appearance = making sure I looked the part when I saw people.*

- *Reliability and contact as life happens = great communication.*

- *Care calls and messages – not about buying – how are you?*

- *My first time as a guest speaker, Avon conference 2025.*

Thank you so much, Geoff – your teachings will stay with me for life, and I am now moving forward in my other businesses and using your methods to give Celebrity Service there too.

You are amazing.

Thank you.

Dawn xx

And here's a report from Dawn's colleague at Avon, Louise Fox…

I've loved working with Geoff – it's brought the passion back to my Avon business and reminded me how much I love working with people and making my customers feel valued.

Here are the things I have done differently. First, my enthusiasm has increased so much. Most of my business is online, but I distribute around 25 Avon brochures monthly to customers I picked up during lockdown. I have really worked on adding the 'personal touches' for my in-person customers. When I drop off their brochure there will always be a sample or gift of some kind. For Mother's Day, I did a little individual wax melt (Avon, of course, which led to some sales), a fragrance sample and a little poem about Mother's Day.

Each month I enjoy thinking about how I can theme my little brochure gift, or if it's a sample I film a little video telling them what the sample is, how they use it and what the benefits are. This has also led to increased sales, as the customer understands it.

When delivering my orders, I will pop in a 'thank you for your order' card with a personal handwritten message on the reverse side. Again, I will also pop in a small gift, usually a sweet of some kind or a sample – something that lets them know I appreciate them! I also now buy my own plain paper bags and use the beauty advisor stickers on them.

For my online customers, when they order from me for the first time, I send them a little video message introducing myself and telling them that I'm a certified beauty advisor and how I can help them with any advice on products. I want to become more than just a distributor – I want to be their point of contact when they want any help with their skincare, and that's exactly what I'm letting them know. Plus, I'm putting a face to the name and building that relationship.

I have always messaged to say thank you when I get an online order, but now I will try to send a voice note and really make my messages personal.

When there are new product launches I'm advising everyone on products and again offering samples to my customers – and they are loving them!

I've also started doing 'get ready with me' lives in my VIP group and giving tips along the way about make-up application – and I know that everyone is loving them too.

Each month, I already create a prize draw for those that shop online with me, to say thank you as I don't have to deliver their orders. I've again been packaging the gifts really nicely, have increased the value of my gifts and popping in a handwritten note, letting them know how much I appreciate them as a customer.

These little things take a bit longer but have made me happier with my business and have definitely delivered increased results. Everything I now do, I ask myself, 'Is that Celebrity Service, or could I do that better?' I'm always trying to think about how I can give people a better experience.

Louise Fox, rep training specialist, Avon

CRAFT BAKERS ASSOCIATION (CBA)

My second CBA conference featured brand new stories and ideas focused around the food sector. However, the CBA team were also in the front row and took the ideas on board for themselves...

Celebrity Service ideas implemented since the talk with Geoff Ramm:

Personalised video content

We've taken Geoff's advice to heart by increasing our use of video, moving beyond generic messaging to personalised, real and engaging content.

Example: We now have a video testimonial from one of our members sharing why they joined the Craft Bakers Association and how it's supported them. Putting a face to the testimonial adds credibility and emotional connection, which has helped in recruiting new members.

Building a press box community feature

We're launching a press box for this year's business day – an exciting new feature inspired by the idea of removing barriers and showcasing the personalities behind the profession.

What it includes: Interviews with members and industry suppliers sharing their experiences, passion for the industry, and why they're part of the CBA community.

Purpose: This brings a human voice to our messaging and reflects the 'celebrity' treatment, making every member feel valued, heard and celebrated.

Community over benefits messaging

One of the most impactful takeaways was the need to communicate the support of the community, not just the list of benefits. We're now focusing messaging on how it feels to be part of the CBA: the support, the camaraderie, the shared challenges and wins – something we're encouraging members to express in their own words through video and at events.

Removing barriers to joining

We've re-examined our communications and processes to ensure there's nothing intimidating or complex about joining. We now ask:

Are our forms simple?

Is our language welcoming?

Are we making it obvious that anyone in the industry can find a place with us?

Business day video promotion

We're using video to promote this year's business day, making the event more dynamic and inviting from the outset. These videos not only advertise the event but also highlight the human energy and enthusiasm that defines the CBA and its members – again, bringing the 'celebrity' spotlight to the everyday heroes of baking.

Key takeaways from Geoff Ramm's talk:

- *Use video more to add personality and visibility to your message.*

- *Create a community, not just a membership.*

- *Show support, not just services or benefits.*

- *Remove barriers – make it easy and inviting to engage and join.*

- *Let members tell the story – their voices are more powerful than our marketing.*

Karen Dear, CEO

BLOOMING MARVELLOUS

One event for the Garden Centre Association to a room full of budding entrepreneurial garden centre owners led to this…

We have a spring huddle every February before the start of the gardening season. We close early on a Sunday and get the whole team together for a celebration of the previous year, a presentation about the coming year, some training and product knowledge about what is new or interesting, a tasting of the new café menus, a test of the new cider/wine/beer from our food hall, etc – then we all have pizza together.

This year, my presentation included a blatantly plagiarised piece on Celebrity Service taken from your presentation. I included the piece on George Clooney and waited with bated breath to see if anyone would shout out his name and, sure enough, after a few minutes his name was yelled from the back by a lady called Sharon.

Since the huddle, we have been talking about Celebrity Service at our 10 to 9 meetings (a daily brief staff chat that includes bite-size product and customer service training). We have produced a crib sheet for the managers to use to encourage everyone to say hello to every customer. This was our first aim – just to get everyone confident to say hello and the rest will follow.

We are encouraging our managers and team members to reward each other when they see someone greeting the customer and talking about Celebrity Service in our twice-weekly company newsletter News and Views *– I attach a couple of copies, which have some nice customer stories and feedback within them.*

Finally, today we received a really touching letter from a customer thanking Sharon (yes, the George Clooney fan!) for her help in sourcing a remembrance rose. Lots more to do, but I think it's a good start and always great to see feedback like this for the team.

Thanks for the inspiration!

Tam Woodhouse, Millbrook Garden Centre

SEEING IS BELIEVING

To kick-start the year, I took a trip north of Hadrian's Wall to Urquhart Opticians. They closed all of their stores and every member of the team descended on Kilmarnock. A half-day Celebrity Service session was delivered and every touchpoint came into focus…

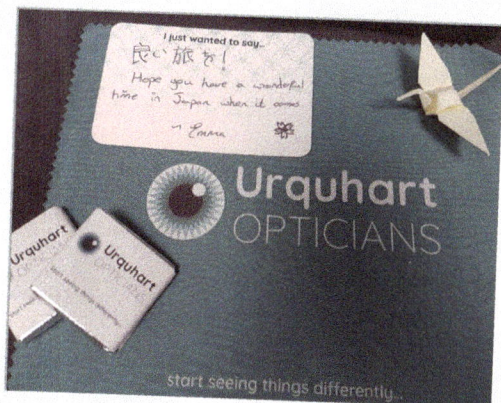

We introduced our Celebrity Service award. Every month, team members nominate each other for the award when they have seen a great example of Celebrity Service. There is a cash bonus and trophy. Some of the winning examples include a team member going to a patient's house to help when his wife called to say he had fallen in the driveway on the way to his appointment.

Kidner Opticians have changed the wording on their posters announcing when they close for training afternoons. They now word it as 'Ideas Brewing'.

We now give everyone a personalised, handwritten 'thank you' card on collection of their glasses. A great example of this was when Emma wrote the card in Japanese when a patient told her they were taking their new glasses on holiday to Japan.

We have a team member called Martin who inserts a patient's eye drops for him as he has no family to do this.

Angie has visited a patient in hospital to fix their glasses. She took some chocolate and sat for a while to have a chat with him.

Cheryl bought a patient a pamper package with her own money as the patient was going through chemo treatment.

Emma collected a patient from Saltcoats and drove them to another one of our stores to be seen for an emergency appointment when the patient had no transport.

Our team in Stranraer regularly send birthday cards, get well cards, etc, to patients who are celebrating big events or birthdays.

We have many team members and optometrists who go over and above to see patients at lunchtimes or stay late to help someone.

We have implemented our 'five touchpoints' to develop our Celebrity Service:

- *Everyone is offered an enhanced eye examination on booking.*

- *Everyone is given a warm welcome and a lifestyle questionnaire.*

- *Patients are taken on time and, if possible, early. If late, we apologise.*

- *Patients are walked to the door and thanked for using Urquhart when leaving.*

- *Every patient is given a personalised 'thank you' card on collection.*

IHG

The latest IHG Hotels & Resorts conference took me to Edinburgh, where the focus was solely on the internal customer – the team.

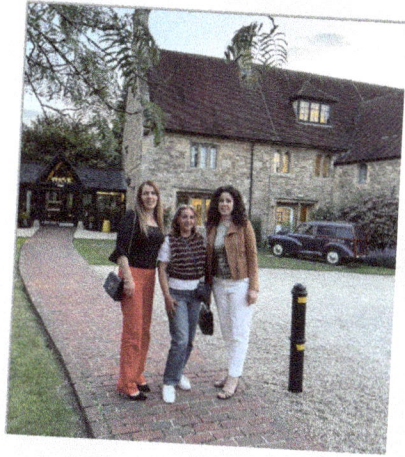

See what we have done in the Oxford Cluster following your fantastic training. The feedback has been really nice and it is good for colleagues to see what we do from a guest perspective. Following the Edinburgh conference, we've been offering a dinner, bed and breakfast experience for all colleagues to redeem at either hotel as a birthday treat.

Best regards,

Georgia Ireson, Cluster HR manager

MEON VALLEY TRAVEL

This was the second time I've worked with the magnificent team at Meon Valley – a travel agency that prides itself on personalised service and doing everything they can for you to have a memorable holiday…

My challenge is… as there's so much… where do we start?

Your presentation on Celebrity Service struck a chord with everybody in the business to the degree that we determined it needed to form the core influence in simplifying our business plan. Starting from the top with the wealth of matters to which Celebrity Service could apply, it was deemed to be important enough to redraft and simplify the business plan so we could embrace all the elements of our awesome business without getting stuck in the weeds. After all, without our customers, where would we be?

Once one has a plan that includes the vision of why we do what we do, it's important to effectively communicate the values of who we are and what we represent and the tone with which we present it. So we defined these as our values and tone documents.

Following the values and tone, one needs a training framework to communicate the story that everyone understands and to which they can contribute.

Furthermore, as we now have 50 per cent of our staff hybrid working from home and office, it's proven crucial that we champion Celebrity Service and cheerlead success. Regular town hall updates celebrate the business wins and our ability to navigate constant change and challenge while remembering to remind ourselves of the good news one customarily forgets.

Two specific examples are as follows:

The Rhodes fires of September 2023. We had a number of clients displaced by the tragic wildfires that spread across Rhodes in the early hours of the morning. Most notably, we received a call at 04:00 from a family who were evacuated barefoot onto the beach to escape peril. Rather than simply rely upon local emergency services, we woke up our people and embarked on our campaign to find a solution to our clients' circumstances.

Roads were closed, public transport shut down, emergency services occupied and all transport stopped. After exploring all options (cars, taxis, hoteliers and staff in safe areas and local representation contactable through the travel ecosystem), we found a water sports centre with a suitable sports boat and a willing owner to leave his family and travel by sea to collect our clients plus any other families they could squeeze on board.

Emergency police and port services were all warning watercraft to stay away from the area but our hero, knowing the local terrain, was able to pluck our clients and another family from the beach and take them to safety. The video of them passing burning hotels at speed across water was something to behold – all while our hero's own house was burning down.

Hoteliers in a safe area came to the rescue, providing accommodation and respite, giving our clients and their companions in safe and secure comfort until they could join their original flights home.

We subsequently established that our hero's five-year-old son was a committed Chelsea football fan, so we arranged a member of staff to hand deliver a match-worn shirt signed by John Terry as a thank-you after the event, to not be forgotten. I'm sure this is just one of many heroic stories from the fires, but it's the one we know.

The second example feels rather self-serving as we celebrate staff success with diamonds each year and a millionaire's trip to Tiffany's in New York for our top performers. Last year (2024) marked our biggest success, with nearly 25 per cent of our staff achieving the goal. Needless to say, we had a fantastic weekend in New York to celebrate and we look forward to what 2025 has to offer.

James Beagrie, managing director

ISLANDS IN THE DREAM – AN INCREDIBLE IHG GUEST EXPERIENCE

Devina Morjaria and I brought Celebrity Service to the EMEA region, first to the IHG conference in Dubai, and from there it was Muscat (and its fabulous airport lounge), then on to Cairo. At each event I changed the stories and ideas to help keep everyone engaged, but the message remained the same for the leaders in the room: 'What could you do for your team and your guests that you would do for an A-list superstar?'

For the Cairo event, Tariq Labib and Ryan Morries sent out a question, asking all of the hotels what they had delivered since the Muscat conference.

We received so many videos, emails and photographs showing how everyone had embraced Celebrity Service, but most importantly they went into detail. During tech rehearsals in Cairo (at the Citystars hotel, where they baked my book!), I chose the overall winner, which was the Intercontinental Muscat, and here's the reason why.

Mr Steels has been a frequent and loyal guest for more than 20 years, so the hotel decided to celebrate and thank him for his loyalty by creating Steels Island near his favourite spot by the pool, making his memories truly special.

PENGUIN MARCHES ON...

Delivering both internal and external experiences all added up for the Welsh teams at Penguin Wealth. Here are some of their highlights following our day:

- *A client came in on his 65th birthday. We reserved his car park space with balloons, brought a cake into the meeting with his coffee, and handed him a card signed by the entire team.*

- *We turned the Penguin office into a Christmas grotto and invited clients and their children, grandchildren, nieces and nephews, to meet the 'real' Santa. The children received age-personalised gifts, there was cookie decorating, crafts and a healthy dose of sugar (plus mulled wine for the grown-ups).*

- *We hosted a 15th birthday party for the firm and celebrated with clients by serving champagne – because what's a milestone without a little theatre?*

- *One team member mentioned wanting to learn to cook international dishes, so we sent him on a cooking course in London to help tick off his bucket list.*

- *We created a quiet breakout room in the office for our team to recharge – their own little VIP lounge.*

TRANSPENNINE EXPRESS

The TransPennine Express train company was about to launch its brand-new onboard catering range across the North East, Yorkshire, North West and Scottish networks.

However, it wasn't just the food that they would be elevating, as they wanted to inspire the crews to deliver a great passenger experience. So the entire catering team attended the Celebrity Service interactive events and before they'd even left the station, the ideas were on track to make them stand out in the marketplace…

Here's a wonderful selection from the team's trolley…

I had the idea to incorporate safeguarding with my passion for dogs due to the multitude of benefits that dogs can have on people's health and wellbeing. With help from the team and working in conjunction with occupational health, my own dog, Nya, was registered and trained as a therapy dog to help staff and passengers with their health and wellbeing. She has now helped hundreds of staff and passengers and been involved in events at Sheffield, Cleethorpes, Manchester Airport and Hull as well as on board the trains. She became the official therapy dog, which made TPE the first train operating company in the world to have its own therapy dog.

Steve O'Callaghan, safeguarding and crime prevention lead, TPE

SHINING STARS

Each period, we want to share some of the amazing feedback we receive from customers across X, postcards and the contact centre.

Travelling to York with my wife on her birthday. Stephen was wonderful – great service with a lovely attitude and created a nice atmosphere in the carriage. He noticed it was my wife's birthday and even gave her a card. Top service – thank you!

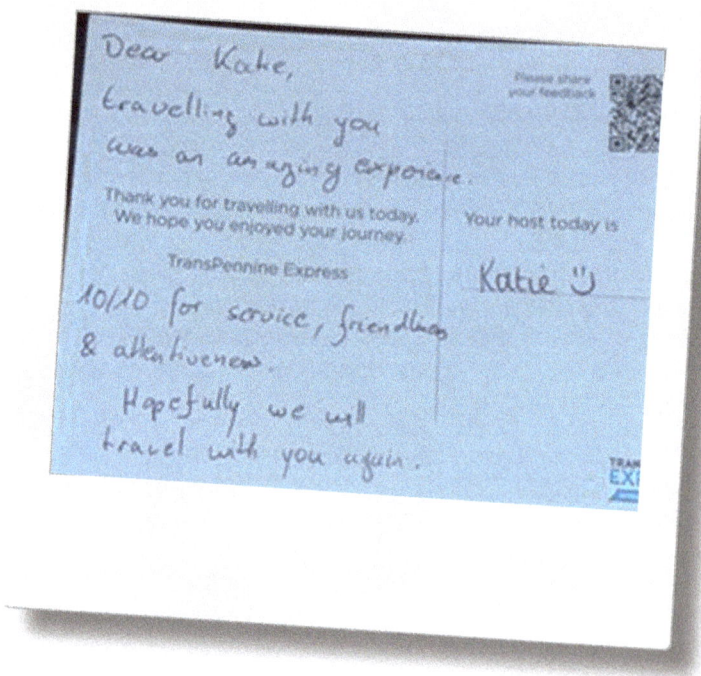

Good morning, TransPennine. What a wonderful journey I've had on the 06:12 train from Chester-Le-Street to Liverpool Lime Street. John Banks looked after me again and he truly makes first class worth every penny! He is so attentive and kind, and makes sure he spoils me with all the first-class goodies on offer on board. This man truly goes above and beyond and he deserves any and all rewards you're able to give him. He clearly has such a passion for his role and it truly shines through – the sun might be starting to come up as the train arrives now that it's summer, but John Banks is the true ray of sunshine! Please make sure this message makes it to him and the management team. He truly is the best! Thank you.

My fiancé and I got on the train from Edinburgh to Newcastle yesterday at 14:10. The guy who brought the snacks on the trolley. I didn't catch his name but he overheard that we were having a baby. We had a lovely conversation about becoming parents as he was also having a child soon. He was the most polite, kind person and also brought us a card to say congratulations and good luck. Please let his manager know what a great person they have working for them. I will definitely be travelling with TransPennine Express in the future due to this interaction.

I'm on the 14:03 from Newcastle, getting off at Manchester soon, and I wanted to give a commendation to Lily, who's 'manning' the refreshment trolley today. It's my birthday and she's been really lovely to chat to. After Lily passed through and I bought a wine (did I mention it's my birthday? No day-drinking judgement, please!), she came back with a card and some snacks. It's made me, and the woman on the table opposite, a bit emotional. What a lovely, thoughtful thing to do! I hope you can pass on my gratitude to Lily and Alex. They're truly wonderful customer hosts.

SEWELLS SUCCESS

Since Geoff delivered a session for our team, they've been absolutely buzzing – always looking out for examples of Celebrity Service and nominating colleagues for recognition. We've changed the way we do things to make interactions with our business more fun and memorable, and the feedback has been fantastic!

Building manager Steve Winsor, who works for our facilities management business, was going about his usual day-to-day tasks of looking after one of our health centres, making sure the building was in tip-top condition and well maintained. He was walking through the car park when a nurse that works at the health centre was stranded due to a flat tyre. Steve duly helped the nurse pump up her tyre and saw her on her way. Steve didn't realise that this was observed by some VIP guests who were there for a tour of the centre – former health secretary Alan Johnson and local MP Emma Hardy, who remarked how wonderful Steve was! It just goes to show, you never know who's watching!

Rachel Smurthwaite, head of communications

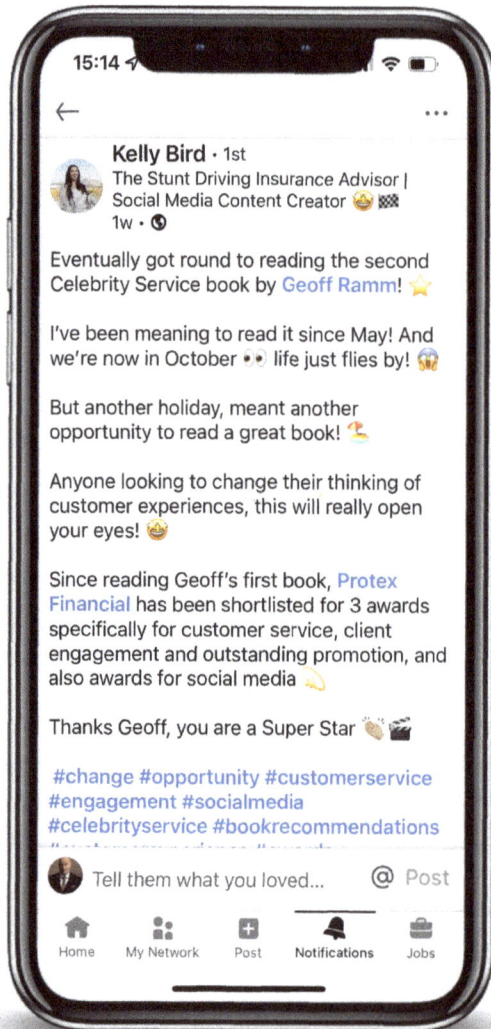

BEDE'S SCHOOL

I'll leave you with this wonderful example of what happened next.

Working alongside inspirational headteacher Peter Goodyer, I returned to Bede's School in East Sussex for a second time to share brand-new stories, ideas and techniques on their inset day.

All of the staff took part in the 120 Challenges to generate ideas to deliver great experiences for their pupils and parents. But there was a twist…

As Peter explained in a subsequent email: 'Regarding the 120 Challenge,one of our boarding houses recently implemented a fantastic initiative. It culminated in a "friend dating" evening designed to help pupils from two of our boarding houses get to know each other. The innovative part was that they were given 120 seconds to speak with each person before moving on. This was a valuable part of our pupil boarding induction programme, successfully helping new boarders integrate and connect with both new and existing members of the boarding community.'

And what happened next…

I am just the messenger. I have more than 700 stories, ideas, techniques and strategies. But it's up to the individual, the team, the brand or the organisation to pick it up and run with it.

Those that embrace Celebrity Service, win.

Thank you to everyone in this section who is continuing to win by changing their mindset, spotting opportunities and taking action like never before…

So...
THERE
YOU GO

CELEBRITY SERVICE SECRET SAUCE

It's the one thing that makes the difference.

It's the smallest of ingredients that completes the experience.

SO WHAT EXACTLY IS IT?

It's listening.

It's reacting.

It's asking.

It's caring.

It's actioning.

It's recognising.

It's celebrating.

It's planning.

It's opportunistic.

It's grabbing every moment and saying…

'I am going to make this better for you.'

'I am going to put a smile on your face.'

'We're going to make this memorable.'

The Secret Sauce is essentially you and your team and the things you will do differently tomorrow.

You are the ones that will drizzle that sweet, delicious ingredient onto your business to bridge the gap in your service you never knew existed.

AND FINALLY...

Thank you for reading this book.

I hope you've been inspired by the stories and maybe muttered, 'Ooh, I love that' once or twice, but most importantly you are excited to implement the ideas from the challenges and can see the opportunities in front of you, for your business and your team.

I'd love to think you're walking away with a handful of ideas.

Let me know. I'd love to hear them.

Take care, best wishes and wishing you every future success.

Geoff

Answers from page 18: 1. Phil Parkinson. 2. Elliot Lee and Paul Mullin. 3. Ryan Reynolds and Rob McElhenney

CELEBRITY SERVICE 2ND EDITION (2018)

Discover an inspiring way to serve like never before. Your customers will love you. Your competition will not.

Inside this book, you will find the answers to set you, your team and your business apart in your industry. From the cabin crew member who gives away prizes, to the restaurant in downtown Philadelphia with knockout entertainments, you'll see how service will always lead to the sale.

You'll find out why five-star service should be outlawed and why one Paralympian continues to inspire the next generation. You'll discover what to do when you can't deliver on your promise and how to offer superb service – even when you're closed!

Geoff will reveal the philosophy, the stories and the award-winning results that have led companies across six continents to outperform their competitors.

'What an absolute delight to read.' – UKTI

'Nothing provides such excellent referencing, true-life examples and a humorous, relevant twist.' – ASAP

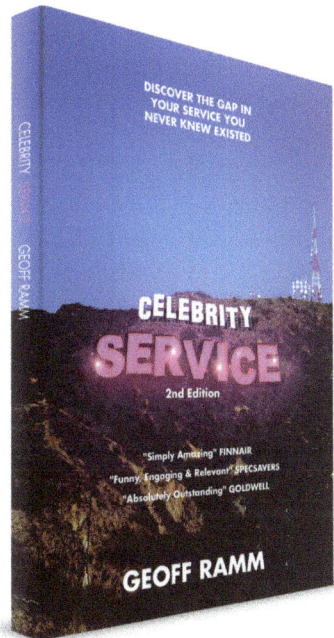

CELEBRITY SERVICE SUPERSTARS (2021)

If you're not being talked about, then you're not delivering an experience that deserves to be talked about.

Geoff Ramm has, in this book, handpicked the most original, unique and quirky examples of creative customer experiences that are guaranteed to inspire you and your team to outperform, outmanoeuvre and stand head and shoulders above the competition.

It's your ticket to service superstardom and it's going to reveal to you:

- smart techniques to help you generate clever experiences of your own

- simple, cost-effective ideas and touches that will mean the world to your customers

- fun, fresh and exciting new perspectives that will inject your entire team with enthusiasm

- fantastic ideas and inspiring stories that will get you spectacular results.

Why not join Geoff on this highly enjoyable, eye-opening and rewarding customer service journey around the world? He'll introduce you to some of the amazing people he's met who have discovered extraordinary ways to deliver world-class experiences, and he'll show you how you can use their strategies to make your own brand unforgettable, your business unmissable and your customers coming back for more.

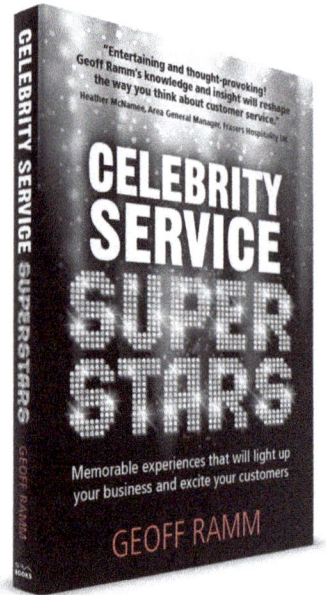

EU Safety Representative: euComply OÜ Pärnu mnt 139b-14 11317 Tallinn
Estonia hello@eucompliancepartner.com +33 756 90241

www.ingramcontent.com/pod-product-compliance
Lightning Source LLC
Chambersburg PA
CBHW041732200326
41518CB00019B/2577